Books Written by the Same Author

Standing on His Promises:
Finding Comfort, Hope, and Purpose in the Midst of Your
Storm

Prayer and Meditation:
Finding Comfort, Hope, and Purpose in the Midst of Your
Storm

Prayer and Meditation for Teens:
Finding Comfort, Hope, and Purpose in the Midst of Your
Storm

Prayer and Meditation:
Biblical Self-Help Tools for Parents of Teens When You Do
not Know Where to Turn

Rise Up

How to Overcome Your Battles Utilizing Faith and Belief in God

Joan M. Blake

To Don + linh
Good health and Blessing
Joan M Blake
1/22/2017

Key to Life Publishing Company
Boston, MA 02119

Dedication

I dedicate this book to my daughter Leah Monique. I will forever be grateful to you for supporting me in ministry and in countless other ways. Thank you for your love and commitment. I love you and pray that God will continue to bless you.

Contents

Acknowledgements

I could not write and finish this book without the support of my husband Carl, who took care of our household while I spent hours working on the manuscript. He suggested ideas for the book cover and helped me as I worked through the contents.

I want to thank my sons and daughters: Anthony, Rese, Leah Monique, Jo-An, and their families for their continued love and encouragement. My family brings laughter and joy into my soul. They are my inspiration as I continue to write these books.

I thank Ruth Hawk for the initial editing, Cherry Gorton for her in-depth insights, Claire Dewey for her general input, and Jill Carrier for reading and editing the manuscript and being available on short notice to edit changes.

I thank extended family, friends, and prayer partners for their continued prayer and support.

I thank God for encouraging me and helping me during all phases of writing this book. I bless Him and will forever be grateful to God for life and zeal. He has taught me endless truths throughout this process: He is God Almighty and that my life is in His hands; no action on my part is necessary to prove His eternal love for me; and my identity is in Him. I thank Him for his direction as He guided me to the stories to use as examples. I can do all things in Christ who gives me strength (Phil 4:13).

Preface

I wrote *Rise Up: How to Overcome Your Battles Utilizing Faith and Belief in God,* to encourage, strengthen, and help men and women of all ages and faiths who are struggling to find purpose in their lives, who feel insignificant, who feel unloved or unwanted, and who feel hopeless because of their difficult past.

Rise Up discusses how to utilize faith by stepping outside your comfort zone while holding onto the truth of God's Word and believing in the supernatural power of God to heal and change your circumstances. These actions cause you to be transformed into that person who understands that your identity is found only in God and that you do not have to perform good deeds to get affirmation from others. When you are transformed, you impact others in positive ways.

Rise Up speaks to your heart from God's heart. God loves you and me beyond measure. Regardless of how we feel or what we have done, God forgives us when we confess and repent of our wrongdoings. Moreover, He has a plan for your life and mine; nothing can negate His love for us.

Rise Up is a spiritual guidebook which you can use for spiritual reflections, for book clubs, for community Bible studies, and for support groups.

I use biblical as well as everyday stories to illustrate God's unconditional love and to encourage readers to love themselves as God loves them; to depend on Him for strength; to help them understand and believe that God has never given up on them; therefore, they can rise from situations which stifle them or keep them in captivity.

To enable easy reading, I have minimized biblical references from most chapters, except for the italicized sections. The italicized sections are revelations that came to me during my prayer time.

I have complied with my family's wishes to use middle name and nickname for my sons and middle name for my younger daughter.

I pray that as you read this book, you will encounter joy from knowing and experiencing God's love. I pray also that your faith will increase as you put your entire life in God's hands and believe in His supernatural power to heal you and change your circumstances.

Chapter 1

Press On

Today is September 12, 2007. I woke up praising and worshiping God. When I think of Who God is and what He has done for me, I cannot help myself. God has showered me with goodness and mercy, has loved me when I did not deserve His love, carried me when I was weak, positioned me as His daughter, and given me life. Do you have days or mornings like that, when you have a song of praise on your lips? I was sobbing uncontrollably, not because I was sad, but because God has been my strength, my joy, my hope, and my strong tower. I can do all things through Him, Who gives me strength (Phil 4:13).

Holding my stomach as if the pain were coming from there, I rolled to and fro on my bed, like a woman in labor, waiting for her baby to be born. I felt the burden of my family and the world around me. I lifted my hands in total surrender to God, Who is in control of everything—even my future. Women who have experienced the pain of labor remember the word "push." When a baby is born, we seemingly forget our toils, our pain and our anguish, for we have brought life into the world.

Similar to the word "push" is the word "press," a term that the Apostle Paul used in his letter to the Philippians in chapter 3 verses 13-14, which read as follows: "Forgetting what is behind and straining toward what is ahead, I press on toward the goal to win the prize for which God has called me heavenward in Christ Jesus." Before his conversion, Paul, the newest of the apostles, lived a life contrary to the will of God—persecuting and keeping Christians in bondage. After his conversion on the Damascus road, God commissioned Paul to serve as an apostle to the Gentiles, changing his name from Saul to Paul.

His life took on new meaning as he lived solely for the glory of God. Paul did not feel guilty, angry, or unforgiving. He had work to do. He pressed on, pushed, released the pain that he felt and brought life to others. During the course of his ministry, he was beaten, stoned, imprisoned, and shipwrecked for the sake of the Gospel, but he pressed on regardless of his sufferings or his past actions. He wrote the Epistles to help build up the early church, and today, his Epistles represent doctrinal truths of the Gospel and the Old Testament which we can study and from which we can learn.

Jesus Christ pressed on knowing that in the three-year span of His public ministry, He would complete His mission on earth by bringing the Gospel message to many, by setting the captives free, by healing the brokenhearted, by giving hope to those who were in despair and by opening the door of salvation and eternal life to those who would believe in Him. The crowds thronged Him everywhere He went. He pressed on, traveling by boat to other regions. At times, He left the apostles and disciples to pray, because He understood that His difficult mission was to die and to pay the price for sin. He pressed on even as He envisioned the gruesome task of carrying the cross to Mount Calvary and the pain and agony that He would experience for the benefit of us all.

You may feel that as a result of your past, you are not good enough to make a difference in the lives of others because people have hurt you. Perhaps you were successful in your business endeavors, but currently, you are facing failures and you do not have the zeal to "press on." Regardless of your situation, when you fail to press on, you choose to remain in a state of captivity and are unable to achieve the purpose God has destined for you. Through the Epistles, the Apostle Paul shares his story and helps us to understand what "pressing on" means. Additionally, God promises through His Son, Jesus, that He will provide for us, that He will be with us, and that He will continually guide us (Phil 4:19; Ps 23:4; Ps 32:8).

Reflect

Hear what the Lord Jesus is saying to you in your present situation:

> *I will give you all that you need (Phil 4:19); Do not become discouraged although you are tried by fire; You will go through fire, but you will not be burned (Isa 43:2); I and the Father are one (John 17:22; John 10:30); I will walk with you (Ps 23:4); I will never leave you or forsake you (Deut 31:8); I will not leave you comfortless; I will guide you with Mine eye (Ps 32:8); My Father will not withhold any good thing from His children (Ps 84:11); Walk by faith and not by sight (2 Cor 5:7); Press on to the mark of the high calling of God in Christ Jesus (Phil 3:14).*

Respond

Do you have a mission to accomplish yet are failing to press on? Describe the reasons for failing to press on.

Chapter 2

Rest in God

You made the decision to "press on," but little did you know that the battle was about to begin. You said, "Lord, I am pressing on, but I can't seem to get anywhere!" Are you resting in God and having peace while the battle is raging, or are you trying to solve your own problems?

The word "rest" signifies the attitude of total trust that a believer should have in God. When you rest in God, you are not anxious about your life's issues, because you have entrusted every area of your life to Jesus Christ. He is the One who fights your battles.

Sitting on a chair in the library as I write on my laptop is an example of resting. I could have chosen to do one of two things: inquire about the make of the chair, its construction, its strength and how old it was or trust that the chair would hold me up. The common practice is to do the last—sit and trust that the chair will hold you up. We rest in chairs at many places, including our homes, at doctors' offices and at restaurants. We utilize simple faith to believe that chairs are sturdy and will hold us up. On the other hand, when we seek God on a certain issue, we continue to feel anxious, as if God did not hear our prayers. We question whether God can and will fix our problems, when He will fix them, and how He will fix them. Resting in God means leaving all the details of our lives in His hands.

We leave things in God's hands because He is the author and finisher of our faith (Heb 12:2 KJV). He is the Alpha and the Omega, the beginning and the ending (Rev 1:8 NIV). In Him, we live, and move, and have our being (Acts 17:28 NIV). He is the One Who knew us before we were born and Who knows our destiny beforehand. He knows what is best for us. So, that problem that you have asked God to handle, He may not fix it in the way you intended or when you wanted Him to fix it. God may solve your problem another way, or He may decide not to solve it. Yet, whether He answers our prayers or not, God remains sovereign.

God has remained sovereign even when I have faced difficult situations. While I was devastated when our son was in prison and when our daughter became mentally ill, I knew that God, Who is all powerful, would make a way for me even when I was hurting. God gave me strength in my situations; He answered our prayers for our son, who was released many years ago and is living a successful life. I patiently wait on God to heal our daughter Jo-An. In my impatience, I have asked God from time to time: "What about Jo-An? She is your daughter. She was brilliant and articulate, and had excellent writing skills, and now look at her! How long, Lord? Will You ever heal Jo-An? How will she make it in this life? How do I teach our daughter when she has lost most of her skills? Where do I go from here?"

These, and other endless questions, plagued my mind, even as her illness helped me to understand God's call for me to work with mentally challenged individuals and others who are disadvantaged. God was not going to answer my prayers when I wanted Him to or how I wanted Him to, nor was my answered prayer dependent on my doing His will. Rather, He wanted me to rest in His comforting arms and leave all the worries to Him. He alone has the answers for Jo-An's life. God is no respecter of persons. He loves

Jo-An in the same way as He loves you and me, and He has a plan for her life.

The above example shows how I was questioning God instead of resting in Him. God is our Father, and He cares for His children. He knows what is best for us. The Bible states that God is the potter and we are the clay. The potter shapes the clay to produce a vessel fit for use in His kingdom. In the same way, God uses our challenges to bring us closer to Himself and uses our unique gifts for His glory. I have prayed more during periods of adversity than at any other time of my life. I know now, that God is the source of my strength; He loves me more than anyone else can, and I can rest in Him.

Reflect

Hear what God is saying to you and me today:

Why are you questioning Me? I formed the earth and everything in it (Ps 89:11); I create light and darkness (Gen 1:3; Isa 45:7); I create the sniper to destroy (Isa 54:16); I am the potter, and you are the clay (Isa 64:8); Can the clay tell the potter what to do? Behold, I make the vessel to dishonor and the vessel to honor (Rom 9:21); I am your God (Exod 20:2); I formed you and fashioned you (Gen 1:27); I brought you up from the miry clay (Ps 40:2); I have a plan for your life (Jer 29:11; Eph 1:11); I am your Creator (Isa 40:28); I will bring these plans to pass; Those whom I love I discipline so the difficulties that you are experiencing are part of my plan to bring you to myself (Rev 3:19), for it is with great love that I love you, greater than the love anyone else can give you (Eph 2:4); You may feel lonely, but you are not alone, for I am with you (Ps 23:4); Rest in me (Matt 11:28).

Respond

What does resting in God mean to you? Are you finding it difficult to rest in God? Why?

Chapter 3

Be of Good Cheer; I Have Overcome the World

*I*n the previous chapter, we noticed that Jesus offered us rest for our souls if we choose to lay down the worries of the world and come to Him. Now, He is offering us yet another promise: "Be of good cheer; I have overcome the world" (John 16:33).

Jesus, in John 16:33, prepared the apostles for the difficulties they would encounter as they preached the Gospel of Jesus Christ. The apostles were sorrowful and confused regarding Jesus' impending departure, but Jesus assured them that He would send the Holy Spirit, the Comforter, the Spirit of Truth, Who would convict the world of sin and encourage hearts to believe the Word of truth by turning them

13

to the living God. Every believer is sealed with the Holy Spirit of promise—everlasting life. Jesus would no longer operate at one place or time, but would, through the Holy Spirit, be everywhere at all times. Jesus also made another promise, that through His death and resurrection, He would sit at the Father's right hand and intercede for those in need (Rom 8:34). Most importantly, the apostles would be comforted by knowing that Jesus had overcome the world by conquering sin and death.

Everyone who followed Christ tended to suffer for the sake of the Gospel. The book of Acts showed that the apostles were not exempt from suffering. You and I also stand to face tribulations in our homes, communities, or workplaces when we make decisions to follow Jesus. The enemy knows that we are children of God and that God has plans for us, plans to use us for the work of the Kingdom, and he would do anything to deter God's plans.

God's plan for Jesus was for Him to die to pay our sin debts in full so that we could have a direct relationship with God. Following His baptism in the Jordan River, Jesus was led by the Spirit into the wilderness, where He fasted and prayed for forty nights. The devil tempted Jesus in many ways, including the temptation of hunger, during which he requested that Jesus turn stones into bread. Succumbing to the Devil's request would have negated the plan that God had for Jesus: to preach, to teach the Gospel, to die on the cross, to rise the third day, and, thus, to bring hope, salvation, and eternal life to all who are lost. Jesus, focusing on His mission, responded, "It is written, that man shall not live by bread alone, but by every word of God" (Luke 4:4 KJV).

Notice that Jesus prayed, fasted, remained intimately connected to his Father, and, in total obedience, submitted to all that God expected of Him. In times of pain and sorrow, we can depend on the Holy Spirit to give us comfort, peace and joy. The Holy Spirit will guide us and give us wisdom to deal with our everyday decisions and life issues. Even when we feel like giving up, we must remember that God is always with us and that we can turn to Him, calling on the name of Jesus.

Reflect

Hear what the Lord Jesus is saying to you and me today:
You are tried by fire, the same way that gold is tried (1 Pet 1:7); A servant is not greater than his Lord (John 13:16); If I have gone through trials, you will too (John

15:20); I died and rose again so that you might have life and have it abundantly (John 10:10 KJV); "Be of good cheer; I have overcome the world" (John 16:33).

Respond

What comes to mind when you read John 16:33? How has your situation changed as a result of this statement that Jesus Himself made?

Chapter 4

Understand That, All Things Work Together for Your Good

When we are going through trials, we do not think objectively or see the big picture, but God knows the beginning and the ending, because He is the author and finisher of our faith (Heb 12:2). We blame parents, siblings, extended family members, and the people closest to us for our circumstances, not realizing that our trials are working together for our good. Let us take a look at the life of Jacob's youngest son, Joseph, to see how this Scripture verse applies.

We read about Joseph in Genesis 37, who dreamt that his brothers would one day serve him. His brothers were already angry that Jacob favored Joseph, so when Joseph told his brothers about the dream, that offended them all the more. The Bible states: "They conspired against him to kill him," but Reuben, their oldest brother, begged them not to, so they threw Joseph in a dungeon which was empty. At Judah's suggestion, they sold Joseph to the Ishmaelites, who in turn sold Joseph to Potiphar, an officer of Pharaoh and captain of the guard.

God blessed Joseph, and he rose to a high position in Potiphar's house (Gen 39-40). Potiphar's wife was attracted to Joseph, and because Joseph did not respond to her wishes to sleep with her, she lied and told her husband that Joseph had tried to seduce her. Potiphar put Joseph in prison, but God had a divine plan—to make all things work for Joseph's good. Joseph received favor and was put in charge of the king's prisoners, including the chief butler and baker, whose dreams Joseph interpreted. The baker was hanged, and the chief butler was restored to his former position, just as Joseph had predicted. Although Joseph asked the chief butler to remember him to Pharaoh, the butler did not remember Joseph until two years later, when Pharaoh had a dream and no magician could interpret it.

Joseph revealed that the land of Egypt would experience seven years of plentiful harvests, followed by seven years of famine. As a result of his revelation,

Joseph became governor in charge of gathering and storing food in preparation for the famine. His brothers came down to Egypt to buy grain, not knowing that they would meet and reconcile with Joseph and bow down before the very person they had sought to kill. Despite the hardships Joseph endured, God's will for Joseph prevailed in the end, as Joseph was the instrument God used to provide for the people of Israel during the famine. God, Who is good and kind, orchestrates our lives and causes situations to work for our good.

Reflect

Hear what God is saying to you and me today:

From this day forward, you will never have to worry, for I will take care of you; I will take care of every detail in your life (1 Pet 5:7); Your house is mine; Your husband/ wife is mine; Your children are mine; Your job, your money, your car and everything that you own are all mine (Ps 89:11); You are mine and I am yours; You will never have to worry about finances, because I will provide for your needs (Phil 4:19); Everything I send into your life from now until you die will be a blessing; Even the things that seem difficult will be blessings, for through them all, I will bring about my will in your life (Rom 8:28); If you suffer from strife, I will bless you with peace (Ps 29:11); If you suffer from hate, I will bless you with love (Eph 2:4); If you suffer from hunger, I will feed you (Matt 6:26); If you suffer from mistreatment, I will comfort you (Isa 51:12); Every circumstance you experience is for your good (Rom 8:28); You must pass the test of time to obtain the crown of life (Jas 1:12); In all these things, the Father, the Son, and the Holy Spirit will be glorified; I am the Alpha and the Omega, the first and the last, the beginning and the end (Rev 22:13 NIV); In me, you live and move and have your being (Acts 17:28); Every good thing comes from the Father above (Jas 1:17); In everything, give thanks, for this is the will of God concerning you (1 Thess 5:18); All things work together for good to those who are called according to Christ Jesus (Rom 8:28).

Respond

How does the story of Joseph help you in your present situation? For example, how will problems in your marriage, in your workplace, in your church or synagogue, with your relatives, or with your children, work out for your good?

Chapter 5

Break up Your Fallow Ground

The passage, in Jeremiah 4, shows us how God called the prophet Jeremiah at an early age to speak prophetically to the nations of Judah and Jerusalem. Despite God's pleas to "put away" their abominations out of His sight, repent, turn to Him, and receive His blessings, the nation of Israel continued to reject Him in order to worship false gods. Jeremiah warned them to "break up" their "fallow ground" and not "sow among thorns." Literally, fallow ground is hard ground worn out by rain or snow, and the only way to make the fallow ground soft is to turn it over, loosen it, and convert it into good soil with the hope of getting plentiful returns. Jeremiah used this analogy to instruct the Israelites to turn their lives around by

21

renouncing false gods, by returning to God, and by receiving His blessings.

We are often like the Israelites in Jeremiah's time: living in the yesterday of our lives, stuck in the mud of fear, unforgiveness, self-hatred, anger, control, resentment, bitterness or whatever seems to trouble us. God will use a prophet or circumstances in our lives to deliver His Word to our hearts.

At the time that I heard "break up your fallow ground," I was remodeling my kitchen, and the contractor was tearing down and replacing walls and floors. Although this was an enormous task, overwhelming and inconvenient, we were happy over the new look and the convenience of the kitchen. In the same way, God is calling us to pluck up those emotions that cause us pain, to repent, and to prepare our hearts for joy and peace. When we are in a state of joy and peace, we can better hear the still voice of God and receive His blessings.

A few years ago, I mentored a woman who felt that God did not love her. Going deeper into her past, I realized that her failure to receive God's love was based on her family members' inability to demonstrate God's love to her. As a result, she sought to please people to get the affirmation that she needed. When she could no longer please others, she felt like a failure and blamed others at her church or elsewhere for hating her. Emotions such as self-hate, insecurity, rejection, fear, anger, resentment, bitterness, and unforgiveness surfaced. She had difficulties confessing, repenting, and uprooting the emotional issues that kept her in bondage. She no longer had the faith and the joy that she once had in God, and she wondered how God could love someone like her.

The past had crippled this woman from understanding God's unconditional love for her. The Bible tells us that while we were yet sinners, Christ paid the price for our sins by dying on the cross. He rose from the dead, victorious over sin and death, so that we could live freely (Gal 5:1). The woman in our story could not think clearly because she was reliving her past. She was allowing negative feelings from her past to rob her of a sense of God's unconditional love. When she uprooted the fallow ground of her past by turning her life over to God, the One Who redeemed us and made us whole, her life became good soil so she could minister to others and reap a great harvest for God's Kingdom.

Reflect

If you are experiencing a similar issue, hear what God is saying to you this day:

> *Your maker is your husband; the Lord of hosts is His name (Isa 54:5); Arise, daughter/son, I will fight your battles (2 Chr 32:8); I will come with a strong arm (Isa 40:10; Ps 89:13), for I am a consuming fire (Deut 4:24); You are holding on to the past because you are afraid that I will make you over into a vessel that I will use; Break up your fallow ground (Jer 4:3).*

Respond

Describe the fallow ground that you need to uproot so you can turn your life over to God.

Chapter 6

Thank God for His Lordship

You made it through 2014. Maybe you didn't obtain everything you wanted, but you got what you needed. You experienced trials that you didn't expect. Perhaps you lost your job, which left you without money to pay your rent or your mortgage. Perhaps, you experienced the painful toil of divorce or separation from your spouse and the downward spiral of your family relationships. Perhaps, you experienced death in your family or difficulties dealing with an adult son or daughter who seems to follow a difficult path. Possibly finding that special person in your life has not been easy, and you feel like giving up. Additionally, you may have been faced with a sudden illness in your family that has put a strain on you.

For example, you may have had to care for an elderly family member or a child with special needs. Maybe being a caretaker has left you drained or you do not have a life of your own. Perhaps, you have prayed, just as I have, and the Lord has been slow in answering your prayers. Let us look at the fate of the Canaanite woman in Matthew 15:21-28, who dealt with her demon-possessed daughter.

Jesus came to Tyre and Sidon, and the woman approached him, crying out, "Lord, Son of David, have mercy on me! My daughter is demon-possessed and suffering terribly." Jesus did not answer the woman, and His disciples wanted Jesus to send her away. Jesus explained to the woman that His ministry was to the Jews. The woman knelt before Jesus and begged for His help, saying, "Lord, help me!" Jesus insisted, "It is not right to take the children's bread and toss it to the dogs." She replied, "Yes, it is, Lord, even the dogs eat the crumbs that fall from their master's table."

The Canaanite woman in our story was a Gentile, a stranger to the commonwealth of Israel, and was considered unclean by traditional Jewish rites of cleanliness. She sought Jesus for healing because she knew that all power was in His hands. She attributed lordship to Jesus by calling him "Lord, Son of David," and, by doing so, made Him her Lord. She cried out for mercy because she knew that, inherent in His character, Jesus is a merciful and compassionate God. She was specific with her request. She wanted Jesus to heal her daughter, who was tormented by an evil spirit; she wanted Jesus to break Satan's power over her daughter. She was not discouraged when Jesus was silent; she remained patient. She did not feel unwanted or angry when Jesus stated that He had come to minister to the lost sheep of Israel. She utilized faith by kneeling and asking for Jesus' help one more time: "Lord, help me."

The woman knew that God is a present help in the time of our need and is always willing to give you and me the help we need (Ps 46:1). She persisted, even when Jesus told her bluntly that He would not take the children's bread and give it to the dogs. Jesus was saying that He had come to minister to the lost sheep of Israel and not to Gentiles, whom the Jews referred to as dogs. Humbly, she beseeched Jesus, ready to take the crumbs from the Master's table. She knew Jesus as the bread of life (John 6:35), Who promises always to give to those who are hungry and to quench the thirst of those who believe in Him. In the midst of discouragement, she rose up. She released her faith, persevered, positioned herself, believed, and expected to receive a blessing from Jesus, her Lord and Master.

When Jesus saw her faith, He said, "Woman, you have great faith! Your request has been granted." Her daughter was immediately healed.

Many times, God will remain silent to test our faith, to see how we are persevering in prayer and how we are trusting Him in all our situations. Even when He appears to be silent, God is listening to our prayers. You may be facing an experience similar to the Canaanite woman's, but, regardless of what your life experiences have been, I want to encourage you to consider God, Who knows the end from the beginning, the All-knowing, All-powerful, Almighty God, Who decided to extend your life and mine today and give us hope.

Reflect

Let us, therefore, make the following personal declarations as we give God thanks:

In the name of Jesus, I have salvation; Lord, I thank You for salvation today (Ps 27:1; Exod 15:2);

In the name of Jesus, I have hope; God, I thank You for hope today (1 Tim 1:1; Rom 5:2);

In the name of Jesus, I no longer fear; Lord, I thank You for freedom from fear today (Ps 34:4; 2 Tim 1:7);

In the name of Jesus, I am delivered; Lord, I thank You for your deliverance today (Ps 3:8; Ps 40:17);

In the name of Jesus, I walk in light and not in darkness; God, I thank You for Your light today (1 John 1:5; Ps 27:1);

In the name of Jesus, every knee shall bow and every tongue confess that Jesus is Lord (Isa 45:23);

God, I thank You for Your Lordship today (Phil 2:10-11);

In the name of Jesus, I have gained a friend; Lord, I thank You for Your friendship today (Luke 7:34);

In the name of Jesus, God has forgiven me; God, I thank You for Your forgiveness today (Jer 31:34; Rom 4:7);

In the name of Jesus, I have courage; God, I thank You for giving me courage today (Josh 1:6, 9,);

In the name of Jesus, I have life, joy, peace, longsuffering, patience, and love (John 14:6; 15:11; 14:27; Col 1:11; 1 Thess 4:9); Lord, I thank You for these gifts today.

Respond

Describe your unique issue here, and list areas where you can thank God.

Chapter 7

Be Committed

Having grown up on the island of Trinidad, I know what it is like to work hard and to be committed to my parents and those in authority over me. Being the oldest, I worked hard in school so I could graduate and obtain a job to help my parents and my siblings. I understood the sacrifices my parents had made to give us children what we needed even to the point of leaving themselves without personal necessities. I showed my parents how much I loved and appreciated them by committing to obey them, by conducting myself appropriately, and by helping them financially. As Christians who have been bought with a price (1 Cor 6:20), we can imitate the Apostle Paul and show God how much we love Him by accepting His commission to tell the Gospel story and to share the love of God with others.

On his second missionary journey, the Apostle Paul met Timothy (Acts 16:1-3), whom he may have trained in the Old Testament Scriptures (2 Tim 3:14-15) and converted on his first visit to Lystra. Knowing that he would die soon, he wrote to Timothy from a Roman prison, preparing him to take on leadership of the churches at Ephesus (1 Tim 1-6). In his letter, he reminded Timothy about his unique faith in Christ and charged him to be strong, to be committed, and not to be ashamed of the Gospel of Christ.

But Paul was not concerned about his sufferings. He wanted Timothy, as well as others, to understand that a true believer or servant of God is characterized by his or her commitment to sharing the Gospel of Christ regardless of his or her circumstances. Christ "has saved and called us with a holy calling," not because of our works, but "according to His own purpose and grace, which was given to us in Christ Jesus before time began" (2 Tim 1:9 NKJV). God's calling is based on His unmerited favor toward us and our destiny, which He planned long before we were born. Paul lived like Jesus. He gave his life for the sake of the Gospel, preaching and teaching to Jews and Gentiles regarding the Gospel of Jesus

Christ. He remained committed in the face of constant beatings and imprisonments until his eventual martyrdom. Devoid of self, he went wherever God sent him. He prayed and worshiped God, even in prison. God was with him throughout his journey and supplied all his needs wherever he went. He trusted God even in the worst times of his life and looked to God as his source of strength.

Jesus Christ, our Savior and Lord, was beaten, forced to carry the cross to Mount Calvary, and nailed to the cross He carried (John 19:17-18). But when He died on the cross, the veil of the temple was torn, and a great earthquake occurred. After His resurrection, dead bodies rose from their graves, and eyewitnesses confirmed that Jesus "was the Son of God" (Matt 27:51-54). Jesus had kept His commitment to die for the sins of humankind, for without the shedding of blood, there could be no remission of sins (Heb 9:22). Jesus became our sacrifice, paying for our sins and conquering death, so we could have life. He rose again the third day and now sits at the right hand of God as our high priest, continually interceding for us (Rom 8:34).

Now, we can go boldly before God and have the assurance that God hears our prayers. We can confess and repent of our sins, obtain forgiveness, and receive

Jesus as Lord of our lives. When this happens, we receive the gifts of salvation and eternal life. Moreover, the Holy Spirit comes to live in our hearts, and, from then on, we are never alone, for He is our helper and guide. Just as God forgave Paul of his past and called him to be an apostle for God's glory, He can do the same for you and for me. God is not a respecter of persons. The same Jesus, who suffered and died, also rose and lives forever and will also bring life to our mortal bodies. Our suffering on this earth is not in vain. We can say, like Paul, "I am not ashamed, for I know whom I have believed and am persuaded that He is able to keep what I have committed to Him until that day" (2 Tim 1:12 NKJV).

The sacrifices and the commitment that I have made for my family — leaving my job before retirement age to care for our special needs daughter, cooking, cleaning, and caring for my family or the commitment that you have made for your family — cannot be compared to the sacrifices that Jesus made for us on the cross. While I have written books and continue to work in ministry, I need to be committed to God's work of sharing the Gospel of Jesus Christ with a heart on setting the captives free.

Reflect

Hear what God is saying to you and me:

I am looking for people who are committed and who will lay down their lives for the sake of the Gospel; I am looking for true worshipers who will worship me in spirit and in truth (John 4:24); I am looking for people who are devoid of self, people who are willing to go higher in me; I will lead you and carry you through this journey (Isa 42:16; Isa 46:4); You will experience rough times, but do not be afraid; Because of your life, other peoples' lives will change; Are you willing to take this risk for Me? Are you willing to go with Me? Are you willing to go where I send you? Look to Me as your source of strength (Ps 46:1).

Respond

In what ways do you plan to commit your life to God? Explain.

Chapter 8

Concentrate on God, Not on Your Circumstances

The Apostle Paul, in Philippians 4:12, states that he has learned how to be satisfied in all circumstances: in times of need and in times of joy. His feelings didn't change because he was experiencing difficulties, and he didn't wait until his situation got better to do God's will. In Galatians 2:20, the Apostle Paul states, "I have been crucified with Christ and I no longer live, but Christ lives in me. The life I now live in the body, I live by faith in the Son of God, who loved me and gave himself for me." His life and faith were rooted in Christ. Let us consider the healing of the beggar in the book of Acts to understand the concept of concentrating on God, and not on our circumstances.

The passage in Acts 3:1-16, tells of a beggar who was crippled from birth, who sat at the gate called Beautiful begging alms as the people passed by. If you and I were to describe this beggar's growing up years, each of us will describe his life differently. The following is how I will describe his life: Because of the difficulties he experienced with other children, his mother kept him at home and cared for him day and night. Feeling lonely and rejected from not having friends and knowing that he could not care for himself and might never walk again, he became depressed. He resorted to begging because he would receive the financial help he needed and build relationships with people as they passed by.

One day, apostles, Peter and John passed by and as the custom with the beggar, he asked them for money. Peter's response was, "Look at us." When they had the man's full attention, Peter said, "I do not have money to give you. In the name of Jesus, walk." Peter took the man by the hand and instantly his feet and ankles became strong and he went with them leaping and jumping and praising God. I believe that Peter asked the man to be quiet so that the man could focus and be attentive to what Peter was about to say and do. When he concentrated on what God could do for him rather than on his circumstances, (his physical and financial state), he was instantly healed.

We concentrate on God rather than on our circumstances because God is the author and finisher of our faith (Heb 12:2). God is powerful and knows everything about us. He sent His Son to die on the cross to set us free. God wants to communicate with us and give us what we need rather than what we want. God wants us to stop begging for things and instead, wants us to worship Him, to praise Him, to thank Him for Who He is. He wants us to have an intimate relationship with Him. When we worship, praise, and thank God and build an intimate relationship with God, we are looking up to God, the awesome God, the God of the Universe, Who can do exceedingly, abundantly more than we can ask or imagine (Eph 3:20).

Reflect

Hear what the Lord is saying to you and me today:

I will go before you and make the crooked places straight (Isa 42:16); I am the Lord; I do all these things (Isa 45:7); Remember not the former things; Behold, I do a new thing in your life (Isa 43:19); Do not be concerned about people and things; The race is not for the swift (Eccl 9:11), but for the one who will hold out and obey all that I command; Behold, I am with you always, even to the end of the age (Matt 28:20); Concentrate on Me and not on your circumstances, for I have a work for you to do that is great.

Respond

Describe the circumstances that have hindered you from concentrating on God. Describe the ways you can concentrate on God.

Chapter 9

---※---

Enter Into a Deep and Lasting Relationship with God

God knew everything about us before we were even born (Jer 1:5); He knows our destiny. He has numbered the hairs on our heads. He knows the steps we are about to take, whether good or bad. He knows where we are going and how we are getting there. He knows our thoughts, whether we genuinely love and are concerned about others. Because we belong to God and we are His, God doesn't want us to struggle, but instead, wants us to enter into a deep and lasting relationship with Him.

When we enter into a deep and lasting relationship with God, we know who we are in God; we know what God expects of us, and we have confidence and assurance that we can endure trials because God is with us. We do not doubt God's ability to bring us out, but we stand firm on God's Word and His direction for our lives. The following examples from the Bible illustrate how God's people stood strong in the face of opposition and how God granted them a greater degree of favor for obeying His instructions.

We learn from the passage in Daniel 1, that Nebuchadnezzar of Babylon took over the kingship of Judah, which was under the reign of Jehoiakim, king of Judah, and that he called for some of the knowledgeable young men of Israel to serve him in Babylon. Daniel and his three friends Hananiah, Mishael, and Azariah (whom Nebuchadnezzar renamed Belteshazzar, Shadrach, Meshach, and Abednego) were among those brought into the service of the king. But Daniel remained unchangeable, refusing to partake of the king's food and wine. He challenged the king's eunuch to compare after ten days his men, who ate vegetables and drank water, to those who ate the king's portions. God gave Daniel favor with King Nebuchadnezzar, who was impressed with the knowledge and wisdom that Daniel and his friends had.

According to the passage in Daniel 2, the king had a dream, and because no magician, astrologer, sorcerer, or Chaldean could interpret his dream, he decided that he would kill all the wise men in Babylon. When Daniel heard the news, he consulted with Arioch, the king's commander of the guard, who coordinated a meeting with Daniel and the king. Daniel needed time to seek God, and when he did, he was able to interpret the dream. Because the king was happy with Daniel's interpretation, he promoted Daniel to ruler over the affairs of the province of Babylon, and gave him authority to place his three friends in leadership positions.

Unfortunately, one day, the king made an image of gold, invited all the leaders of Babylon to the dedication, and instructed everyone who heard the sound of the trumpet to bow down to the image or risk being thrown into a fiery furnace. Word got to the king that Daniel's three friends were not bowing down to the golden image, and after confirming this fact, the king immediately instructed his men to throw Shadrach, Meshach, and Abednego into the fiery furnace. To everyone's amazement, God was with them and saved them from death. Their hairs were not singed, and their clothes did not smell of smoke. Nebuchadnezzar blessed God and was convinced by this incident, that the God of heaven was able to do the utmost when one trusts in Him (Dan 3).

The passages, in Daniel 5 through 8, describe how God granted Daniel continued favor under King

Belshazzar, the son of Nebuchadnezzar, king of Babylon, and also under kings Darius and Cyprus. Daniel
became a great leader who interpreted dreams. But
Daniel was not exempt from trials. Under King Darius,
(in Daniel chapter 6), certain of the king's men envied
Daniel for his leadership. They could not find anything
to complain to the king about, so they urged the king
to sign a decree that anyone in the next thirty days who
submitted either to his own god or to any human other
than the king would be thrown into the lion's den.
Daniel remained unmovable and continued to pray to
God three times per day. As a result, he was thrown
into the lion's den. However, because of his faith, the
lions did not tear him into pieces, for God was with
him. The king believed in God because of Daniel's
faith. At the king's command, the men who had set the
trap for Daniel were thrown into the lion's den along
with their families, where the lions tore their bodies
into pieces.

Like Daniel and the three Hebrew boys, we learn
understanding, wisdom, and confidence from our deep
and lasting relationship with God. When we remain
at the center of God's will, God reveals secrets to us
and our faith increases, allowing us to stand on God's
promises regardless of the trials we bear. We know that
God is with us, and He promises never to forsake us.

Reflect

Listen to what God is saying to you and me right now: *My light shines in the darkness, and the darkness cannot overshadow it (Ps 18:28); You are My daughter/ My son; I have not forsaken you (Deut 31:8); Pray and fast; I desire that you do this; Do not listen to others for direction, for I will be your guide (Ps 32:8); When you go through trials, I will be with you (Ps 23:4); Enter into a deep and lasting relationship with Me (Dan 9:3-4).*

Respond

Where are you in your walk with God? How do you respond when you are tested and tried?

Chapter 10

Love Others the Way God Loves You

few years ago, I was discussing "love" with two of my nieces, who agreed that it is difficult to love those who have hurt you, misused you, and slandered you. We reasoned that the after effects of this pain are deep-seated feelings of anger, fear, resentment, and unforgiveness toward the person who has caused the pain. As a result, you may never reinstate a relationship with the person who has hurt you. I believe that failing to deal with these underlying issues produces inner turmoil that affects relationships in other areas of your life.

This inner turmoil can alter how you deal with new relationships, such as with a spouse, a friend or a co-worker. Instead of loving someone unconditionally and forgiving him/her for the wrongs he/she has done, you may tend to experience and transfer former negative feelings of fear, anger or unforgiveness to new relationships. For example, growing up, our parents did not encourage us to discuss our problems and our feelings. As a result, we kept things in and harbored deep-seated anger. This anger could transfer to new situations such as dealing with a spouse, children, and extended family. Rather than dealing with issues face to face when they occur, it can be tempting for us to sweep them under the rug, only to find ourselves angry at our children or spouses for little things because we have not faced the real issues.

I believe that family members or parties in dispute should resolve their issues by discussing them openly. In cases where they are unable to resolve major issues, having a mature and seasoned family member, pastor, or trusted friend listen and moderate discussions will help parties arrive at viable conclusions. Meeting face to face clears the air, opens up opportunities for discussion, and helps to rid parties of anger and resentment which can hinder them from moving forward. When I have gone to God with an issue and I do not have peace about the issue, then I am angry, and I have to deal with the anger in order to move forward. God makes a way for you and me to deal with, and overcome, our emotional battles. Let them go. Release them, so you can rise to where God wants you to be in Him.

If you are dealing with anger or bitterness toward an individual who is alive or deceased, I believe that you should seek God in a spirit of repentance, forgive the person, and put the situation to rest. You need to forgive that person and move on because there is nothing that can separate you from God's love, for God loves you with an "everlasting love." The Bible states, "This is love: not that we loved God, but that He loved us and sent His Son to be an atoning sacrifice for our sins" (1 John 4:10 NIV). God's love is so infinite toward us that He sent His Son Jesus to die sacrificially to redeem us from our sins, so we can have second chances, ask for forgiveness, receive salvation and have eternal life. God commands us to love one another, for "love is of God; and everyone who loves is born of God and knows God" (1 John 4:7 NKJV). We cannot claim to be reborn and yet hate or dislike another person. God is pleased when we live in unity and love. You may be troubled over the issue of love today. God is speaking to you particularly and wishes that you deal with this so you can live an abundant life.

Reflect

Listen to what God is saying to you and me today:

Make love your aim; Love unconditionally; Continue in My love, for love covers a multitude of sins (1 Pet 4:8); I am calling you to love others as never before; Love your family members and those who have done you wrong; Your love will break strongholds (1 Pet 4:8); Love the stranger on the street, the drug addict, the homeless, the prostitute, the gambler, the thief, and the murderer; Above all, love your enemies; Love the ones who hate you and misuse you; Love is the greatest gift; If you love Me, show Me by loving others (1 John 4:21).

Respond

Describe issues that you have regarding loving others. When and why did these issues occur? How do you plan to change your behavior?

Chapter 11

Trust in God

At 10 am on Thursday, March 2, 2006, I was devastated after listening to a voicemail message from one of my sisters that stated that my niece's husband was fighting for his life. He had been shot while attending a funeral of a dear friend. How could this be? Six weeks before, we had attended their beautiful wedding celebration.

I could not focus on the things that I had set out to do that week. I was praying on the phone with my niece and sister, encouraging them, and holding them up before the Lord. In a state of confusion, I made two attempts to go to the hospital, once when it was pouring rain and another time when it was really late, but I just could not find my driver's license. I decided to go to the Lord in prayer and leave all my burdens with Him. The Lord directed me to passages in Psalm 18 and other Psalms, which I recited to my niece on the telephone. He also inspired me to write a short message for my niece to read to her husband, although he was in a coma. On Friday of that week, I felt truly blessed as I met and socialized with a group of women from the church I attended. On Saturday morning, I went straight to my bureau drawer and pulled out a purse that I had used the previous week. My driver's license was right there!

Although my extended family was depending on my prayers, God was in control of this man's situation, and his fate rested with the Lord, not with me. On the day that I arrived at the hospital, my niece's husband was scheduled for surgery. My sister, my niece, and I prayed, and the surgery was successful. After my niece's husband spent several months in rehabilitation, God, who is the author and finisher of our faith (Heb 12:2), restored him.

All we need to do is to pray and trust God in all situations. God hears our prayers at any time, at any place, even during our worst times. You or your family member may be faced with a life or death situation. Pray and turn the situation over to God. Trust God, and leave all the worries to Him. God's perfect decision will be accomplished in the life of your loved one.

The following example from the book of Ruth teaches us how we can trust God even in our worst times. Naomi, Ruth's mother-in-law, mourned the death of her husband, Elimelech, and her two sons, Mahlon and Chilion; the family had moved to Moab because of the famine in Bethlehem. Naomi was moving back to Bethlehem and discouraged her two Moabite daughters-in-law, Ruth and Orpah, from accompanying her, but Ruth refused to leave Naomi (Ruth 1:8-14).

After Ruth and Naomi reached Bethlehem, Ruth learned of Boaz, a wealthy landowner in Bethlehem, who was a kinsman of Elimelech, Naomi's late husband. Ruth gleaned in his fields and gained his respect and favor. Boaz loved Ruth and wanted to make her his wife. His first step would be to contact the next of kin, referred to as a "guardian-redeemer," who redeemed a relative experiencing difficulty. In the presence of his elders and others, Boaz, himself a "guardian-redeemer," inquired whether the next of kin was interested in securing the property and acquiring Ruth, but the next of kin declined and completed the transaction by removing his sandals, a custom in that day. Boaz purchased the property and acquired Ruth, that "the name of the dead would be remembered with the property" (Ruth 4:9-10). Boaz married Ruth, and they had a son, whom Naomi cared for.

This biblical account teaches us how Ruth trusted God. She activated her faith in God and showed faithfulness to Naomi, her mother-in-law, when she accompanied her to Bethlehem. She knew that God would care for both her and her mother-in-law.

Ruth embraced the qualities of a Proverbs 31 woman. She watched the affairs of her household by deciding to support her mother-in-law. She utilized wisdom by picking up the leftover wheat in the field with the thought of finding favor from Boaz. Ruth did not eat the bread of idleness; she expected God to respond favorably to her as she gleaned in Boaz's field day by day. Ruth knew that she could trust in a loving, caring, faithful, and compassionate God. In the end, God provided for both her and Naomi far more than they had expected. We learn from Ruth that we can exercise our faith by expecting God to act. There is nothing too hard for God. What He did for Ruth and Naomi, He will do for you and for me. He is the same God yesterday, today, and forever (Heb 13:8).

Reflect

Listen to what God is saying to you and me today:

> *Trust in Me; Do not lean on your own understanding (Prov 3:5); You are worried about so many things that you have neglected to trust Me; I feed the birds of the air (Matt 6:26) and in the winter, they find a resting place; Do not worry about your life (Matt 6:25); Help others in these last days to know Me as their personal Savior.*

Respond

Do you have a decision to make regarding someone who is hospitalized, in a coma or are you wondering how God will solve a difficult issue? Describe the struggle(s) you are facing.

Chapter 12

———————❧———————

Be Pliable in God's Hands

The Webster's dictionary defines "pliable" as "supple, flexible, workable enough to bend freely or repeatedly without breaking, yielding readily to others, complaisant or adjustable to varying conditions." Clearly, we are not objects, but when we study the above definitions, we can apply them hypothetically to our lives, especially during difficult times. Some of us bend to the point of breaking and giving up, while still others go through life's pressures, adjusting to "varying conditions," knowing that God will provide the needed strength for the battle ahead.

Queen Esther shows us how to be pliable in God's hands. Chapter 2 of the book of Esther describes a beautiful, young, orphaned Jewish girl who was brought up by her cousin Mordecai. This girl, Esther, was taken to the palace because of King Xerxes' desire to interview young maidens and select one as his wife. Under the care of Hegai, the custodian for the women, Esther received favor, and Hegai "provided her with more beauty preparations beyond her allowance." These beauty preparations were in the form of various oils, with which Esther would prepare herself for one year as a prerequisite to appearing before the king. In addition, Esther was assigned choice maidens and the best place in the palace.

Esther had gone to the palace at a critical time in Jewish history, when the Jews who were carried away by King Nebuchadnezzar of Babylon were returning from captivity and rebuilding their lives (Ezra 1-2). Mordecai advised Esther that revealing her Jewish identity would ruin her chances of becoming queen. The Bible states that the women were all given opportunities to go before the king, but when Esther's turn came, the king was delighted with her beauty, loved her more than the other women, and made her his wife at a great banquet celebration (Esth 2:17). But Queen Esther's position as queen did not alleviate the troubles that she was about to experience.

Mordecai informed Esther of everything that he had learned, and she, in turn, told the king that two men were planning to assassinate him. The king hung the men and recorded the information concerning Mordecai's faithfulness to him in the book of chronicles (Esth 2:21-23). Later, because Mordecai would not bow before the king's minister, Haman, he, with the king's permission, issued a decree to kill all Jews on the twelfth month. When Mordecai learned of it, he informed Esther that she was not exempt despite being the queen, for she herself was a Jew.

Esther, understanding how serious the problem was, called her people to fast and pray for three days and decided to go before the king. Esther knew she was risking her life, for no one appeared before the king without his invitation and lived, except when the king held out the golden scepter to accept that person. Esther was so committed to her decision, however, that she boldly declared, "If I perish, I perish" (Esth 4:15-16). When Esther approached the king, he held out the golden scepter to her, and Esther invited him and Haman to a banquet she had prepared. The king promised to give Esther anything she wanted, but Esther delayed her request until the second banquet (Esth 5:1-7). At the second banquet, she waited for the king to ask about her petition, and she then informed the king of Haman's desire to kill the Jews, including herself. The king hanged Haman and promoted Mordecai to a high position in the palace, and although the decree to kill the Jews had become law, the king protected the Jews from those who could potentially harm them (Esth 8:11).

We observe from the above discussion that Esther possessed leadership qualities. She was a woman of purpose, motivated, decisive, people focused, kind, genuine, compassionate, courageous, tactful, humble, and confident. She was obedient and able to adjust to varying situations. Under Hegai, she prepared herself for one year before appearing before the king. When Esther learned of the possibility that she, along with the Jewish people, would be annihilated, she recognized her purpose—that God had positioned her in the palace "for such a time like this," so she knew there was no time to break under pressure. Esther activated her faith, rose up, and became the woman God had positioned her to be. She became motivated, decisive, kind, genuine, compassionate and loving toward her people while being "pliable" in God's hands. She responded favorably to her people instead of ignoring their pleas. She called a fast and prayed to God for three days. She knew God would answer her prayers and those of her people. She exercised faith by risking her life when she went before the king without his invitation. She knew that God was with her and that

He would protect her from all harm. She used timing to put the blame where it belonged, on Haman, the king's minister. She did everything with humility, tact, and confidence. We can imitate Queen Esther, who knew her identity in God, knew her purpose, and was focused on accomplishing her task.

Reflect

Hear what God is saying to you and me today:

I plan to stretch you beyond what your naked eye can see (Isa 54:2), but you must be pliable in my hands (Jer 18:6); I care for you and know what is best for you (I Pet 5:7); Do not exact pressure on yourself; I will direct you and position you in the areas that I have planned for you (Ps 32:8).

Respond

Are you positioned for God to use you? Are you pliable in God's hands? Can you stand up under pressure, or do you break when the pressures of life overwhelm you? Describe a present situation in your life that is overwhelming or a situation that you have already dealt with. What strategies do you think will be/have been helpful?

Chapter 13

Ask and You Shall Receive

*J*esus often used this phrase throughout His public ministry. "Ask and it will be given you" is a command with a promise. Promises are fulfilled according to God's will, but if we do not ask, we will not receive.

We ask in the form of prayer. Whether you are overburdened with problems, depressed, or oppressed, you should go to God in prayer. Get someone to pray with you when you feel overwhelmed. Seven of our family members met to pray on Friday, July 10, 2015. We affirmed God's power; we learned that God fights our battles (2 Chr 20:15); that He is always with us; and will never forsake us (Deut 31:8). We need to pray at all times and put our trust in God.

The Lord Jesus Christ in Matthew 6:9-13 (NKJV), tells us how we should pray:

"Our Father in Heaven, hallowed be Your name,

Your Kingdom come, Your will be done, on earth as it is in heaven,

Give us this day our daily bread, and forgive us our debts,

As we forgive our debtors,

And do not lead us into temptation,

But deliver us from the evil one,

For Yours is the Kingdom and the power and the glory forever, Amen."

We observe that the first and last lines of the Lord's Prayer are exalting God, the Creator of heaven and earth, and are reaffirming His Name, His ownership, His Kingdom, His power and His glory. The second line asks that God's will be done, not our will, and affirms that it is already being completed in heaven. The prayer also asks God to make provisions for us, to forgive us our sins as we forgive others, and to deliver and protect us from temptation.

Prayer is approaching God in a spirit of worship, magnifying Him for Who He is and what He is all about. God is pleased when we honor and give Him the glory that belongs to Him. We should be in awe as we recognize and affirm the One to Whom we are praying—the Holy One, the Mighty God, the Great

I Am, the Creator of heaven and earth, the source of life, the source of our strength, our Healer, our Deliverer and our Sustainer. We recognize that we can do nothing without Him and that our earthly existence is dependent on Him.

We should come to God in prayer asking for what we need. In Mathew 7:9-11 (NKJV), Jesus says, "Or what man is there among you who, if his son asks for bread, will give him a stone? Or if he asks for a fish, will give him a serpent? If you, being evil, know how to give good gifts to your children, how much more will your Father, who is in heaven, give good things to those who ask Him!" As parents, we give our children the basic things of life, including food, shelter and clothing, and, at times, we go beyond the basics and give our children/grandchildren more than they need. Similarly, God, our Father, is waiting patiently for us to ask Him for what we need so He can provide for us, His children.

We should also ask God specifically for what we need by going to Him in a spirit of expectation, knowing that He hears us and answers our prayers according to His will. In Matthew 20:31-34, we learn of two blind men who sat by the roadside and cried out to Jesus, "Have mercy on us, O Lord, Son of David!" But Jesus wanted them to be specific in their prayers, so He asked them, "What do you want Me to do for you?" They replied, "Lord, that our eyes may be opened." Jesus responded by healing them of blindness. This example teaches us that we should be specific with regards to our requests to God and believe that God will grant our requests.

When God chooses not to answer our prayers, we should respond as King David did and not question God, because God answers prayers according to His will. King David was a man according to God's own heart (Acts 13:22). God blessed him by allowing him to be king over all Israel and Judah. God protected David from King Saul, because David was God's anointed one, the one God had chosen to be king of Israel. After becoming king, David committed adultery with a woman named Bathsheba, the wife of a soldier in his army, named Uriah. When she conceived, David had Uriah put in the front row of a battle, knowing that Uriah would be killed. Then, he proceeded to make Bathsheba his wife. After Bathsheba bore a son, the boy became ill. Although David fasted and prayed for his son's recovery, the boy died, and David once again ate and ceased from worry, for he said: "While the child was alive, I fasted and wept; for I said, 'Who can tell whether the Lord will be gracious to me, that the child may live?' But now he is dead; why should I fast? Can I bring him back again? I shall go to him, but he shall not return to me" (2 Sam 12:22-23 NKJV). God's will prevailed in King David's situation. This unanswered prayer could have resulted from King David's actions surrounding his marriage to Bathsheba.

Notice also that answered prayer is contingent upon an individual forgiving another, for Jesus Himself said in Matthew 6:14 (NKJV), "For if you forgive men their trespasses, your heavenly Father will also forgive you." Pray, believe and forgive others, even those who have wronged you.

Sometimes, God will require you to perform an act before answering your prayer. In the Gospel according to John, Jesus spat on the ground, made clay, anointed the eyes of a blind man, and said to him, "Go wash in the pool of Siloam" (John 9:7). The blind man's healing was contingent on his washing in the pool of Siloam. We hear of people's finances being restored when they give their last penny to a cause. I listened to a Christian television show on which a woman testified that while she was in the hospital, she called in and gave all that she had. Unknown to her, someone had paid the woman's hospital bills in full, a sum that she was unable to pay.

Reflect

Listen to what God is saying to you and me right now:

I have heard your cries, and they have come up before Me, even unto my ears (Ps 18:6); In an acceptable time, I will save your household and provide for your every need (Phil 4:19); Hold unto My unchanging hands; I have not deserted you (Deut 31:6); You are my child (Rom 8:16;1 John 3:1); I am your God (Exod 20:2); Wait on Me; Humble yourself before Me, and I will exalt you; I have need of you, but your sin of pride has come between you and Me; Repent and turn away from your sin, and I will forgive you; I have allowed you to operate in a dry land, where no water is, so you can turn to Me; I have loved you before the foundation of the world, and I have a purpose for your life (Jer 31:3;Jer 29:11); Do not worry about the things of this world; I am the way, and the truth, and the life (John 14:6); Walk before Me and obey my commandments and I will heal your land (2 Chr 7:14); Do not be anxious about anything; Each day has enough trouble of its own (Matt 6:34 NIV); My grace is sufficient for you, for My strength is made perfect in weakness (2 Cor 12:9 NKJV); Depend on Me for all things, for I own the world and everything in it (Ps 89:11); Wouldn't I give you all that you need

(Phil 4:19)? Why are you worrying? Wouldn't I guide you into all things (Ps 32:8)? Don't I know your situation? Am I not your Father (Rom 8:15)? Don't I know what is best for you? Aren't you under My supervision? Lean on Me; You have not because you ask not; Ask Me for help and I will give it to you; Ask and you shall receive; knock and the door shall be opened unto you (Matt 7:8).

Respond

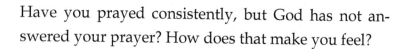

Have you prayed consistently, but God has not answered your prayer? How does that make you feel?

Chapter 14

Stand Firm on God's Promises

Standing firm on God's promises means exercising faith, believing in God's Word, putting your total trust in God and being patient as you wait on God. Waiting means trusting and believing in God's ability to keep His promises that He made to you and me through His Word. Regardless of how difficult your life and mine may seem, we can stand firm on God's promises.

The writer of Hebrews explained in Hebrews 11:6 that he who comes to God must believe that He is and that He rewards those who diligently seek Him. In other words, if you seek God, you must believe in and know Who God is and understand His characteristics. God is the Lord of Heaven and Earth, and all power is

71

in His hands. He is loving, faithful, compassionate and dependable. Regardless of how you feel, God loves you, will never leave you, and will give you a second chance. He knows your destiny, for He is the author and finisher of your faith (Heb 12:2).

The Old Testament account of God's covenant with Abraham brings out this point fully. God assured Abraham in Genesis 15:4, that his servant would not be the heir to his estate but that his own child would be instead, and He promised Abraham that his descendants would be like the stars in the skies. Sarah felt that God was making an impossible promise, seeing that she was past the age of childbearing. As a result, she decided that her maid Hagar would bear a child for Abraham instead (Gen 16:1-3).

We learn from the passage in Genesis 17:5-8, that God made a covenant of circumcision with Abraham. "As for me, this is my covenant with you: You will be the father of many nations. No longer will you be called Abram; your name will be Abraham, for I have made you a father of many nations. I will make you very fruitful; I will make nations of you, and kings will come from you. I will establish My covenant as an everlasting covenant between Me and you and your descendants after you for the generations to come, to be your God and the God of your descendants after you. The whole land of Canaan, where you now reside as a foreigner, I will give as an everlasting possession to you and your descendants after you; and I will be their God."

God also said to Abraham in Genesis 17:15-16, "As for Sarai your wife, you are no longer to call her Sarai; her name will be Sarah. I will bless her and will surely give you a son by her. I will bless her so that she will be the mother of nations; kings of peoples will come from her." While God would also bless Ishmael, Hagar's son, and make him increase in numbers into a great nation, the father of twelve rulers, God confirmed that He would "establish" his covenant with Isaac, the son Sarah would bear for Abraham, the following year. Abraham was 100 years old, and his wife Sarah was ninety years old, when their son Isaac was born.

But the story didn't end there. When Isaac grew up, God instructed Abraham to take the boy to the land of Moriah and sacrifice him on one of the mountains God would show him. Abraham obeyed God and was preparing to sacrifice his son when God told him not to hurt the boy. Abraham's willingness to obey God at all costs showed God that Abraham revered Him. He was truly God's servant. He remembered God's love and faithfulness toward him and was confident that he could stand on God's promises.

Nineteen years ago, I prayed for God to completely heal our daughter Jo-An, and I continue to stand on God's promises for her healing. God continues to work things out according to His will and purpose. Instead of having anxiety, I utilize faith by rising up and helping others who are going through similar struggles. I leave all decisions in God's hands; He can see the road ahead and knows whether to take a different route if the journey gets complex. God's light of love illuminates the darkness of our journeys and gives us hope when we feel like giving up.

Reflect

Hear what God is saying to you and me right now:

Do you know that I love you with an everlasting love (Jer 31:3)? I will make a way for you, for I am your God (Isa 43:19; Isa 43:3); All I want from you are your praises; I want you to be saturated in My love; You will never feel insecure, for My love satisfies all of your needs and wants (John 3:16); I am the Lord; I change not (Mal 3:6); I am turning things around for your good (Rom 8:28); Stand firm on My promises; I will not let you down; I am a faithful God (Deut 7:9).

Respond

Describe a situation in which you struggled to stand on God's promises.

Chapter 15

Remain Focused

Remaining focused is necessary as we journey through life. Being a wife and mother and caring for a special needs daughter, I know too well that tending to general household duties can easily take up most of my time and distract me from achieving my purpose.

For forty years, the Israelites journeyed through the wilderness, but most of their elders did not make it to the Promised Land. They complained about not having water or food; they worshiped false gods and were disobedient to God. They lost focus. Even Moses, their leader, who interceded on their behalf, did not make it to the land of promise. When the Israelites needed water, God instructed Moses to take his staff and to speak to the rock so water would gush out. Instead, Moses hit the rock twice, and water came out of the rock, enough to satisfy the people and their animals. Because Moses did not glorify God in front of the people, God did not allow Moses and his people to enter the Promised Land (Num 20:7-12).

After Moses' death, Joshua, the son of Nun, responded to God's call to be Israel's leader. Joshua had walked with Moses and witnessed the many miracles God had wrought through him. God promised Joshua that he would cross the Jordan River with all the people and would possess every land that they trod, from the wilderness to the great sea. God encouraged Joshua to "be strong and courageous" and to "be careful to obey all the laws My servant Moses gave you." God affirmed Joshua's call by stating, "As I was with Moses so I will be with you. I will never leave you or forsake you" (Josh 1:5).

Joshua, reminding the people of God's promises (Joshua 2-5), exercised faith by sending two spies to explore the city of Jericho. Rahab, a prostitute, hid the two men in her home. In exchange for their safety, the men promised Rahab that she and her entire household would be saved when the Israelites secured the land. The men confirmed to Joshua that the Lord had surely given the Israelites the land He had promised them.

Joshua listened attentively to and obeyed God's instructions. When they crossed the Jordan River, he allowed the priests who were carrying the Ark of the Covenant ahead of the people, to dip their feet at the water's edge, and to stand in it. When they did so, the waters of the Jordan were cut off, and the priests stood on dry land until the multitude had crossed over. Joshua selected twelve men, representing the twelve tribes of Israel, and directed each one to take a stone from the River Jordan. These stones were to remind future generations that God had enabled the Israelites to pass through the River Jordan and the Red Sea on dry land.

Joshua positioned himself and his army for battle exactly as God had instructed him. The armed guard went ahead of the seven priests, who blew the trumpets, and the rear guard followed the Ark of the Covenant. The entire army marched around the city once for six days and, on the seventh day, they marched around the city seven times. On the seventh time, Joshua instructed the army to shout. The walls to the city fell down, and they conquered the city of Jericho, just as God had promised.

Listening to God, following His instructions, and staying focused were God's ingredients for Joshua to win the battle. One of the ways we can remain focused is by praying. God's Word reveals that "The effectual prayer of a righteous one avails much" (Jas 5:16). Prayer enables us to talk to God and listen to His instructions directly.

Reflect

Listen to what God is saying to you and me today:

Hold fast to My sayings; Do not turn to the left nor to the right; Remain focused; I will carry you (Isa 46:4); I will lead you (Isa 42:16), for I am your God (Isa 43:3); Pray unceasingly, My daughter/My son, for times are difficult; You must go through trials for the sake of My Gospel; You will be tested and tried (Jas 1:2), but hold on to the end; I have not given you a spirit of fear, but of power, and of love and of a sound mind (2 Tim 1:7); Be diligent; The devil roams around to see whom he can devour (1 Pet 5:8), but pray and be steadfast, abounding in everything for My sake (1 Cor 15:58).

Respond

What has God been telling you as you listen attentively to Him during your prayer time or when you read His Word? What comes to mind?

Chapter 16

---❖---

Seek God

I once listened to a song by Michael W. Smith which states, "Seek God and you will find Him; when you find Him, just love Him." Let us delve into the meaning of seeking God.

I believe that seeking God is knowing who God is and having an intimate relationship with Him. You and I seek God by crying out to Him in prayer knowing that He is always listening and that He answers prayer. Other ways of seeking God are through worship and by reading and studying God's Word, the Bible. When you seek God, you begin to understand His true character, which includes His love, His mercy, His compassion, His kindness, His goodness, His faithfulness, His gentleness, and His patience.

When we seek God, we will find Him. He is waiting and knocking at the door of our hearts. He is gentle toward us and gives us free will. The more we seek God and the more we concentrate on Him and not on our circumstances, the more we learn about Him, what He requires of us, and how we can please Him. Our attitudes and overall focus on life change over time, and our will comes into agreement with God's will. The following biblical tale of Hannah, the Prophet Samuel's mother, teaches us how to seek God.

In the passage, 1 Samuel 1, we read of Hannah, the wife of Elkanah, who was barren. Every year, she and her husband visited Shiloh to worship and make sacrifices to the Lord in the presence of Hophni and Phinehas, Eli's sons, who were priests. Hannah's rival, Peninnah, had children and, knowing that Hannah wanted children, intimidated and provoked Hannah until she became troubled and grieved over her barrenness. Hannah vowed that, if God blessed her with a son, she would honor God by having her son devoted to the work of the Lord.

One day, Eli witnessed Hannah praying silently and diligently before the Lord, moving her lips but not uttering a word. When Eli approached her, she explained that she was not drunk, but that she was seeking God about her situation. Eli comforted her by saying, "Go in peace, and may the God of Israel grant you what you have asked of Him." At this, Hannah felt confident that God would grant her the desires of her heart. God did; Hannah gave birth to Samuel. This story shows us that even with troubled hearts we can come before the Lord. God knows what is troubling us, but He wants us to confide in Him. Like Hannah, we should seek God with all of our hearts. He is waiting patiently to hear from us so He can help us. God is honored when we seek Him in everything, even in the small matters.

Reflect

Listen to what God is saying to you and me today:

Seek Me with your whole heart and soul; Those who seek Me will find me (Matt 7:7; Luke 11:9); Do not be deceived, for God is not mocked; Establish your faith; Hope in Me; I promise to deliver you from your troubles; I am your deliverer; I am your Savior and your God (Ps 18:2; Isa 43:3).

Respond

Write a letter to God explaining your situation.

Chapter 17

---※---

Forgo Guilt, Regrets, Anger, Jealousy, Unforgiveness, and Burdens

*I*n 2014, I attended a conference which was held in the Boston area. The conference, which was very informative, was aimed at making the community aware of the needs of those who are mentally challenged and those who had been released from prison.

I listened as one woman talked about her growing up years, during which time she was a victim of sexual abuse. Some of her family members were drug users and were incarcerated. She followed in their footsteps by abusing drugs, and she finally ended up in prison. As a result, she was forced to give up her two older children to foster care while her younger children were placed in the care of family members. When she was released from prison, she visited her children and was saddened that the people caring for her children made her feel like an outsider by the remarks they made to her. Her children, who were in the care of uncles/aunts, faced abuse similar to what she had experienced while growing up.

She discussed her feelings of guilt and regret for abandoning her children because she could not get her life together. She was angry at her family members for abusing her as a child and subjecting her children to the same abuse. She expressed feelings of anger toward people in the social justice system for ignoring her pleas to regain her children, and for offering her housing that they intended to take away from her after two years, an action which would hinder her from being self-sufficient enough to reclaim her children. She became jealous and unforgiving toward the adults who took care of her children, since she no longer had the legal right to do so. She was unforgiving to extended family and friends and spoke about her decision to cut them off as she set about to put her fragmented life back together. She spoke loudly, blaming others for her mishaps.

I listened to this woman, and, while she could justify why she felt the way she did, I felt that her healing would only come through forgiving others. Although she had turned to God, the Father, Who had given her strength, and even though she had a community of believers who stood with her, I sensed that this woman needed therapeutic help to defuse her inner turmoil and the fear she was experiencing—fear of her future.

Whether your story is similar or dissimilar to the above story, you have hope. Jesus was delivered to death for your sins and rose from the dead for your justification (Rom 4:25). It was by grace that you were saved, not by any works that you have done or plan to do (Eph 2:8). Our Lord's actions gave you and me unmerited favor—forgiveness of our sins. Now, you and I can go to God in faith, confessing and repenting of our actions, and He hears our cries. When you believe in Jesus Christ and accept Him by faith as Lord and Savior of your life, you receive salvation and eternal life (John 3:16). God no longer sees your sins, present, past or future. You have been washed by the blood of the Lamb, forgiven, and set free. Your sufferings now produce perseverance. Perseverance brings about character, and character, hope. "And hope does not put us to shame, because God's love has been poured out into our hearts through the Holy Spirit, who has been given to us" (Rom 5:3-5). Regardless of who you are or what you have done, God loves you. I want to encourage you to put your hope in Jesus Christ. He will restore you (Joel 2:25). He will put your feet on solid ground and establish you (Ps 40:2), but you must believe, by faith, that He will do it.

Reflect

This is what the Lord Jesus is saying to you and me today:

Forgo guilt; I have forgiven you of your wrongdoings; By My stripes you were healed (1 Pet 2:24); Renew your mind; Behold, I have brought you from the miry clay and have planted your feet on solid ground (Ps 40:2);

Forgo regrets; Put your past behind you and live; Live to Me; Remember when you were sick in the hospital and you didn't know if you would make it, I gave life to you (Ps 103:3); Get busy for Me; I am getting ready to change your circumstances; You must pray and believe;

Forgo anger; Remember, I said, "Let not the sun go down on your anger" (Eph 4:26);

Do not let the evil one have that much power over your mind; Peace, I give to you;

Forgo jealousy; No two people are alike; I give to each person his or her own portion; I will give you what you need in due season (Phil 4:19); All is well;

Forgo unforgiveness; A new command I give you, love one another; As I have loved you, so you must love one another (John 13:34-35); Love all, regardless of how they have treated you; When you make the decision to love and to forgive others, you experience freedom that you have not felt before; When you forgive others, your Father in heaven will forgive you (Matt 6:14), and your prayers will be answered;

Forgo burdens; Come to Me you who are burdened; I will give you rest (Matt 11:28); Burdens only weigh you down, and you can't hear My voice; Find time to read and study my Word; It is a lamp to your feet and will guide and keep you (Ps 119:105).

Respond

Describe your inner turmoil. Why do you feel this way? Give your burden to the Lord and live in freedom.

Chapter 18

Live Anew

The English dictionary describes the meaning of "anew" as "again," "once more," and "in a new way." Living anew means living again or living in a new way. The Bible talks about renewing one's mind in Romans 12:2: "Do not conform any longer to the pattern of this world, but be transformed by the renewing of your mind."

The Apostle Paul was not asking us to change the important things that we do in the world, such as working, attending school or college, operating our own businesses, driving our cars, taking the subway, attending public meetings, being stay-at-home parents or taking our children to sports activities. Rather, he was referring to a mindset that we should adopt as children of God. We should show our gratitude to a God who has showed us mercy by forgiving us, saving us, and transforming us from children of darkness to children of light.

When we were children of the world, we lived in darkness and lived by worldly standards – pleasing ourselves and not pleasing God. The Apostle Paul listed areas that are considered worldly. These areas include fornication, strife, hatred, envy and witchcraft. As children of God, we sometimes struggle with maintaining our freedom in Christ, and we have to renew our minds daily, focusing on the fruit of the Spirit, which includes love, joy, peace, longsuffering, gentleness, goodness, faith, meekness and temperance. We renew our minds by dying to self and taking on a Christ-like attitude.

When we release the fruit of the Spirit that is discussed in Galatians 5:22-23, we live in newness of life. In John 15:5, Jesus said, "I am the vine; you are the branches. If you remain in Me and I in you, you will bear much fruit; apart from Me you can do nothing." The branches cannot operate apart from the vine. For a tree to produce good and abundant fruit, the tree needs sunlight, pruning, and nourishment. Similarly, we are like that tree; we need to possess good soil (the Word of God and a change in lifestyle) so we can produce good fruit. This fruit includes showing love to others by being kind and forgiving and cultivating relationships by our caring and by our giving. When we have love, we release joy. A tree that bears good fruit is full of strength; the joy of the Lord is our strength. When we have love, we experience peace, longsuffering, kindness, goodness, faithfulness, gentleness, and self-control. The Lord Himself tells us in Colossians 3:12 that, as "God's chosen people holy and dearly beloved," we should "clothe" ourselves with compassion, kindness, humility, gentleness, and patience. For example, if you and I are unforgiving, bitter or hateful toward another person, we do not have love. If we desire to have an intimate relationship with Jesus Christ, we must die to ourselves and renew our minds. The Bible questions our love for God if we do not love our sister or brother, whom God loves. Also, God loved you and me even when we were at our worst, so we should do likewise, and love our neighbor.

Maybe you have not forgiven yourself for your past, and as a result continue to live in fear. The Bible states that God has not given you a spirit of fear, but of power, and of love, and of a sound mind (2 Tim 1:7). God, through His Son, Jesus, put to rest all your fears when He died on the cross and rose for your victory. Now, you can live in total freedom and not be bound by fear. Regardless of your past sin, it is never too late to allow God to turn your life around. Ask yourself this question: "Am I pleasing God by living this way or under these conditions?" The answer should come quickly. "No." Confess, repent, ask God to forgive you, and turn away from the situation you are in before it consumes you. God is able to bear the weight that you are carrying. Be transformed by the renewing of your mind.

Reflect

Be comforted as you listen to what the Lord Jesus is saying to you and me today:

I know all of your pains, your sorrows, and your troubles; I took them to the cross where I was nailed to death (1 Pet 2:24); When I died, your pains and sorrows died also; You are no longer in bondage to your pains and sorrows; Live anew; Live a life of joy, for I have already taken care of your burdens; With zeal, I carried the cross on my back; When I fell, I got up and continued on my way to Mount Calvary so I could set you free; I know the weight you are carrying is heavy, but you do not need to carry it any longer; I will carry it for you

(Ps 68:19); Only be My vessel to bring the Gospel message to the ends of the earth; Pray continually and maintain your focus; Do not lean on your own understanding; Consider Me in everything; It's not about you, It's about Me; Let me do what I set out to do in you.

Respond

Describe why you feel unforgiving, bitter or resentful toward another person (name the individual). Discuss ways you can live anew.

Chapter 19

March to Win

Have you ever wondered why God created you? He created you for a purpose, and He had a plan in mind when He created you. Believe in yourself and in the God who created you. His plan will come to fruition in your lifetime.

Moses' birth and life help us to understand how God's plan comes to fruition. Moses was born when Pharaoh, king of Egypt, ordered all Hebrew boys to be slaughtered. Pharaoh wanted to prevent the Israelites from multiplying further and becoming a great nation. Jacob's sons and their generations had settled in Egypt as a result of the famine in Canaan. New generations of Israelites had multiplied in the land of Egypt, and the king of Egypt felt threatened by their fruitfulness.

When Moses was born, his mother hid him in a basket made of pitch and clay and laid him among the reeds in the Nile River (Exod 2:3). Pharaoh's daughter discovered Moses but wanted Moses' mother to nurse the child for a time before taking him. At the acceptable time, Moses grew up in the Egyptian culture, but he remembered the Hebrew people. He killed an Egyptian for hurting a Hebrew. Later, when he scolded a fellow Hebrew, that person reminded Moses that he had killed an Egyptian. Terrified that others might hold him responsible for the murder, Moses left Egypt and settled in the land of Midian, where he married Jethro's daughter (Exod 2:5-23).

God's plans for Moses began to take shape when He appeared to Moses in a burning bush and explained that He had heard the cries of the Israelites (Exod 3:2-10) and that He would use Moses to lead the people of Israel from Egypt to the Promised Land of Canaan. Moses was uncertain whether he could carry out that great mission. He made excuses to God about his stammering and insecurity, stating that people would not believe that God had sent him. God showed him that He (God) would put the words in his mouth and use the staff in his hand to break through the hardened heart of Pharaoh. We learn from the book of

Exodus that God used Aaron, Moses' brother, to speak to Pharaoh and used Moses' staff that Moses used, to bring about several plagues in Egypt (Exod 4:14-17; 7:1-2). The staff was also used to allow the Israelites to walk on dry land and to cause the Egyptians and their chariots to drown in the Red Sea (Exod 14:21-22, 29).

Even when the Israelites complained in the wilderness, God was faithful. He guided them as they traveled through the wilderness, providing a pillar of cloud by day and a pillar of fire by night (Exod 13:20-21). God also gave them manna (a light, flaky crust) in the desert when they did not have food to eat (Exod 16:14-15). God was faithful to His promise to bring the Israelites to victory, but they had to move from their state of oppression and rise to new heights. They had to march to win.

Similarly, you must rise from your bondage and seek your freedom. Only when you rise up will you take a step toward victory. Don't think of getting out of your situation alone. You are not alone, for God is with you (Ps 23:4). When you take the first step to freedom, God will send others to your rescue. You take your first step by acknowledging that you need help. If your need is great, seek help. Call on God. He will help you right where you are. Go to a Bible-believing church where you can hear the Word of God. Go to a recovery center where people can help you. Call on a close friend or family member who will listen to you and help you find the assistance that you need.

Reflect

Listen to what God is saying to you and me today:

You feel insignificant, but I am a big God (Jer 32:17); I use insignificant people so I can show people how big I am (1 Sam 17:33-36); I am the Holy Spirit; I will fill a room if you allow Me to enter in (Acts 2:1-2); I am Jesus, who sacrificed Myself on the cross for your sins (1 Cor 15:3); I desire to sup with you and tell you My plans (Amos 3:7); Do not confuse My plans with your plans; My plan is to use you for My glory (Jer 29:11; Acts 1:8); Do not be afraid; As I used Aaron as a mouthpiece for Moses (Exod 4:30), so I would use you as My mouthpiece; Pray vigilantly; I will answer your prayers (Ps 81:7; 138:3); I am not a God who is slack concerning His promises to His servants (2 Pet 3:9); As soldiers in an army, march as a sign of victory; March to win, for the battle is not yours, but Mine (2 Chr 20:15).

Respond

Are you living in a state of bondage and needing to rise from it? Describe your circumstances. Bondage could include being a victim of domestic violence, living in spiritual darkness, and living with emotions such as fear, anger, and a sense of abandonment.

Chapter 20

Run with Your Vision

A vision originates when there is a need. The first chapter in the book of Nehemiah discusses his vision: to remove the disgrace that the Israelites faced by re-building the Jerusalem walls. Nehemiah, a cup-bearer to King Artaxerxes, was instrumental in making his vision a reality.

Under Babylonian rule, some of the key Israel-ites were exiled to Babylon. Under Persian rule, King Cyrus issued a decree allowing the exiles to return to their homeland, Jerusalem (Ezra 1:2-4). They returned only to find that the gates had been destroyed by fire and the walls had been broken down. Let us discuss how Nehemiah went about his mission.

The first point of interest is that Nehemiah,

worried about the situation, first prayed to God. He confessed, repented, and asked God to forgive His people for their rebellion and for their worship of false gods. He reminded God of the promises He had made to them, that if they would repent, He would gather them from all nations and bring them back to the place He had promised them. After making requests of the king, Nehemiah received letters from the king to take to the governors of Trans-Euphrates who would provide for his safety in Judah and to Asaph, the keeper of the forest, who would supply timber for the gates of the temple, for the city wall, and for the residence that Nehemiah would be occupying. Nehemiah prepared for the task knowing that God would keep His promises by providing for his needs.

The second point of interest is when Nehemiah arrived in Jerusalem, he went by night and examined the gates and the ruins for himself before telling the priests, nobles, and officials about his plans (Neh 2:15-16). When you have prayed to God and have received a vision to accomplish a certain project, it is best not to share that vision with someone else until the appropriate time.

The third point is that Nehemiah appointed a team to rebuild the walls, for he could not do it alone. Every vision needs a team working together to accomplish its mission.

The fourth point is that Nehemiah faced opposition from many people, including regional governors serving under the King of Persia such as Tobiah, an Ammonite, Sanballat, a Horonite and Geshem, an Arab (Neh 4:1-3,7), as well as some of the Jews, who doubted whether the work would ever be finished. Nehemiah gave the burden to God and finished what he had set out to do: to rebuild the Jerusalem walls. He refused to leave his duties to speak with enemies. Nehemiah believed that God would fight his battle, for the battle was not his, but God's (2 Chr 20:15).

The fifth point is that Nehemiah remained faithful to his vision, allowing half of the workers to be armed with swords, spears, and bows while the other half did the work. Those who carried materials did it with one hand and held a weapon in the other. Each builder wore his sword at his side (Neh 4:13, 16-17). We learn that Nehemiah and his team completed the rebuilding of the walls in the face of opposition.

In summary, Nehemiah utilized actual swords, spears and bows to protect his men from attackers. In the Epistle to the Ephesians 6:11-18, the Apostle Paul advises us to put on the whole armor of God as a protection against the enemy. As believers and children of the most High God, we have received spiritual weaponry from God which we need to put to use. Knowing that God's Word is true, we can refute all the lies that the enemy brings. We use the breastplate of righteousness against the enemy to remind ourselves that we are righteous and that Jesus paid the price so we could have a right relationship with God. We believe in the Gospel of peace, and our shield is our exercise of faith with which we counteract the perils of darkness that the enemy sends our way. The helmet of salvation is proof that we have been saved by the blood of the Lamb and are secured by God. Lastly, the sword of the Spirit is the Word of God which we utilize in our prayers so we can become overcomers.

Do not feel overwhelmed when you have not accomplished your vision. Fulfill your vision in steps. When our daughter Jo-An became mentally challeng-ed, I was completely consumed by her care. I began working at my ministry in steps. I started a community newsletter which included an editorial and articles written by various community members. I conducted monthly and yearly breakfast meetings, preached and engaged participants in discussion. Now, I am writing books and blog articles. While I may not have realized my vision in its entirety, I have made steps toward my vision. God will guide you and me as we step out in faith.

Reflect

God is saying to you and me today:

> *Stand up to the task; Do not be weary in well doing, for in due time you will reap if you do not faint (Gal 6:9); Every good thing comes from your Father on high (Jas 1:17); I will not withhold good things from you if you walk uprightly (Ps 84:11); Run the race looking to Jesus, the author and finisher of your faith (Heb 12:2); Run to win; Run with your vision.*

Respond

Have you had a vision lately, but stumbling blocks seem to keep you from realizing it? Explain your stumbling blocks and what you need to do to realize your vision.

Chapter 21

Hold on; Do Not Give Up

From the passage in second Kings 4:8-37, we learn of the faith of a Shunammite woman who held on and did not give up. She was a great woman, influential in her community, who set a room aside for the prophet Elisha during his visits to Shunem. Elisha wanted to bless the woman because of her kindness to him, so he had his servant ask the woman what she needed. The servant noted that the woman was childless and her husband was old. Although the woman did not believe Elisha's prophecy that she would have a baby, at the predicted time she gave birth to a son. However, her child died once he had grown a little older.

The woman was not discouraged, however. Instead, she held on to God's merciful hands. Accompanied by her servant, she journeyed to Mount Carmel to speak with Elisha. Elisha saw the woman from afar and instructed his servant, Gehazi, to find out what the woman needed. She did not tell Gehazi of her need but approached Elisha and reminded him, "Did I ask you for a son? Didn't I tell you 'do not raise my hopes'?" Elisha gave his staff to his servant and instructed him to run ahead and place it on the child's face. However, when Gehazi did so, the boy did not respond. Refusing to be slighted, the woman stood beside Elisha until he decided to return to her home. Elisha stretched out on the child, and the child became warm, then he stretched out again, and the child sneezed seven times and opened his eyes. Gehazi called the Shunammite woman, and Elisha presented her son to her.

You and I learn from this story, that the Shunammite woman had consistent faith in God and trusted that He would act on her behalf. God had used the prophet Elisha to speak into her life. God had blessed her with a child, and He would bless her again by bringing her child back to life. When her son died, she rose quickly to get to the prophet whom God had sent. There was no time to sit and weep. She utilized faith by rising up and believing God, and she obtained what she wanted.

Whatever your need is, I want to encourage you

to hold on to your faith. Do not give up. God keeps His promises. I continue to hold on, believing God for my daughter's healing; I will not give up. You can do the same. God promises in Mark 11:23 NIV, "Truly I tell you, if anyone says to this mountain, 'Go, throw yourself into the sea,' and does not doubt in their heart but believes that what they say will happen, it will be done for them."

Reflect

The Lord Jesus is saying to you and me today:

Take heed My daughter/My son; Look at My life; You read the Gospel about how I suffered, bled, and died so you can have life (Rom 5:17); Although I suffered by the hands of cruel men, My love remains unconditional (John 3:16); You, too, must suffer and experience tests (John 15:20); Only in going through times of testing can you truly be My disciple; Since I was victorious on the cross, I have gained victory for you; You do not have to go through these trials alone, for I am always present with you (Ps 46:7); Hold on; do not give up; I will lead you (Isa 42:16); I will help you (Ps 46:1); You are Mine (Isa 43:1).

Respond

What do you want your Father in heaven to do for you? Are you believing God for a child or healing of a child? Are you believing God for the salvation of your children/grandchildren/other?

Chapter 22

Speak God's Word and Apply It to Your Situation by Faith

Driving at night has become challenging for me because of the glare from oncoming cars and insufficient light in general. When I need to drive at night, I consistently speak the Word of God and apply it to my situation by faith. Oftentimes, I recite 2 Timothy 1:7, which states that God has not given me a spirit of fear but of power, and of love, and of a sound mind, and then I pray for God's guidance during my journey. When I pray and speak these words, I believe that God will protect me and guide me safely to my destination, although the enemy would have me think otherwise. Let us consider the story of the Roman centurion found in the Gospel according to Luke 7, who spoke the Word and applied it to his situation by faith.

When Jesus was in Capernaum, a Roman centurion sent his elders to inquire whether Jesus would heal his servant, who was dying. As Jesus was approaching his house, the centurion sent messengers to tell Jesus that he felt unworthy to receive Him. Jesus only needed to, "say the word" and the centurion's servant would be healed. The Roman centurion himself was a man with authority, with soldiers and servants obeying his orders, so he knew he could trust Jesus, who has authority over people and the circumstances they face. The messengers returned and found the servant healed. The servant received healing because the centurion expressed faith in the healing power of Jesus, who has authority over every disease. By asking Jesus to say the word and believing that the servant would be healed, the centurion believed that the spoken word would be applied to his situation.

That Word is Jesus Himself. He was the Word from the beginning (John 1:1). He was with God, and the Word was God. The Word of God is powerful. "The word is settled in heaven" (Ps 119:89). Whatever is spoken on earth is heard in heaven. When we speak God's Word, we are bringing heaven down to our situation. The Word of God is a lamp to our feet and a light unto our path (Ps 119:105). When we speak the Word, we live in conformity to the Word.

Reflect

Hear what God is saying to you and me today:

Daughter/Son, I have heard your prayers; Satan wants to sift you like wheat, but I have come to give you abundant life (John 10:10); You can't afford to get depressed now, for you are in warfare; Defeat the enemy with love and kindness; Conquer, by staying focused in prayer and the task you are called to do, never wavering; Hold on to My unchanging hands; Acknowledge Me in all things, and I will direct your path (Ps 23:2); Remember, you are an overcomer in Christ, Who died on the cross and forever sits at My right hand interceding for you (Rom 8:34); In due time, you will see the rewards of your labors (Gal 6:9); Hope that is seen is not merely hope (Rom 8:24); Speak the Word of God and apply it to your situation by faith; Preach the Word in season and rebuke using the Word (2 Tim 4:2); Be blessed, My daughter/My son.

Respond

Explain why you believe that Jesus has authority over every circumstance and that you can apply the Word of God to your situation by faith, whatever it may be.

Chapter 23

Obey God's Commandment to Love Him and to Love Your Neighbor as Yourself

We show God how much we love Him by obeying His commandments, which are listed in Exodus 20. These commandments were given to Moses and written on a tablet for the Israelites to live by. They are still relevant for us today. I am focusing, however, on the verses taken from Matthew 22:37-40 NIV, where Jesus said, "'Love the Lord your God with all your heart and with all your soul and with all your mind.' This is the first and greatest commandment. And the second is like it: 'Love your neighbor as yourself.' All the law and the Prophets hang on these two commandments."

Jesus was summarizing the commandments by saying, in essence, "If you love Me, you will obey Me and treat another person with love; you would not do things that are not in keeping with My Word, such as stealing, committing murder, committing adultery, and bearing false witness against your neighbor."

Loving the Lord with all of our hearts and minds is, therefore, the first commandment. The second is to love your neighbor as yourself. These two commandments are played out, for example, in our homes, in our workplaces, in our churches, in our synagogues, in our worship centers or anywhere we interact with others.

At home, although some of us have to deal with difficult situations, how we choose to deal with our spouses and family members reflects how we love and obey the Lord. We can choose to be humble in our dealings with our spouses and family members instead of being argumentative and angry. Dealing with children calmly teaches them to be calm, open, and respectful to parents.

In our workplaces, we can choose to interact with our co-workers with courtesy, kindness, and love. Getting away from gossiping by having an open mind toward co-workers, is best. Responding to your boss with humility instead of anger shows that you respect authority, love God, and respect His Word.

Showing respect and love to your elder, pastor, teacher, evangelist, bishop, priest or rabbi, as well as any person with whom you work or sit next to in a church or synagogue reflects the love that you have for God and for your neighbor.

Allowing someone else to get in front of you when you have the right of way on the road shows kindness to your neighbor. One day in June, 2015, while accompanying my daughter on a walk, I fell and could not get up, but a kind stranger helped me. Her help was an expression of her love for God and for me, her neighbor.

The parable of the Good Samaritan, found in Luke 10:25-37, sums up the idea of loving God and loving one's neighbor. A man on his journey from Jericho to Jerusalem encountered robbers who took all that he had, beat him, and left him on the sidewalk to die. Everyone passed him by, including a priest and a Levite, but he/she did nothing to help the man. A Samaritan passed by, had compassion for him, put him on his donkey, and brought him to an inn, cleaned him up, and paid the innkeeper for the man's stay. This act shows that the Samaritan loved God and had love toward his neighbor.

At times, we disobey one or more of God's

commandments. We are told that God forgives us of our sins when we confess and repent of our wrong-doings (1 John 1:9). The term "grace" means "unmerited favor," which is a favor that we do not earn through works and one that we do not deserve. It is a gift of God (Eph 2:8-9). Unmerited favor resulted when God sent His Son, Jesus Christ, to die on the cross to pay our sin debt in full. Now, we have the opportunity to go before God, confess, repent of our sins, and ask for His forgiveness in the name of Jesus. God wipes away our sins and never looks at our past. Where sin is evident, grace is present even more. The fact that we receive an abundance of grace does not give us the liberty to purposely sin. God sent the Holy Spirit to live in our hearts, to guide us on how to live in holiness. We live holy lives to please God for what He has done for us. God's commandments are laws put in place from the Old Testament to help us stay on track.

Reflect

Hear what God is saying to you and me today:

"For I know the plans I have for you," declares the Lord, "plans to prosper you and not to harm you, plans to give you hope and a future (Jer 29:11 NIV); You have

not obeyed My commandments, to love Me with your whole heart and to love your neighbor as yourself (Mark 12:29-31); Pour your love on your loved ones and everyone with whom you interact; When you do so, the doors of heaven will open, and I will send blessings your way (Matt 6:14).

Respond

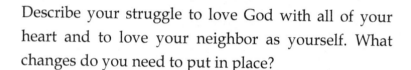

Describe your struggle to love God with all of your heart and to love your neighbor as yourself. What changes do you need to put in place?

Chapter 24

Depend on God for Your Ministry Needs

I believe that everyone is called to do God's will here on earth. Whether you are a layperson, an apostle, a prophet, a pastor, an evangelist, or a teacher, God needs you for the building up of His Kingdom.

When God calls you and me to do a task, we sometimes question His calling for the following reasons: We feel that we do not have that special talent; We feel that the vision that God has given us is too big; We feel insignificant or feel that we do not have the provisions necessary to do the task. What we fail to understand is that God orchestrates the vision and we are simply the instruments God uses to do the work. Whether we have a talent or not, we can minister to others.

There are many ways we can minister to others: by our personal giving, by our contributions and volunteering efforts to other ministries that are already doing the work, through our local churches, or through our own ministries. God has called us to minister to many, including the poor and needy, the homeless, the mentally ill, young girls who are caught up in sex trafficking, and others who are lost and do not know how to reach Jesus, Who is the Way, the Truth, and the Life (John 14:6). We are God's mouthpieces, His hands and His feet. He is depending on us to preach the Word in season to those who are lost, to feed the hungry, to go to the uttermost parts of the world or wherever we are, and to take the Gospel message of God's love to those who are living in darkness and to bring them to Jesus Christ, the Light of the world (John 8:12).

Knowing what is expected of us is one thing, but doing the work consistently by depending upon God for our ministry needs can be quite challenging depending on our circumstances.

While I have written books and have conducted some workshops and women's retreats for the glory of God, I have not been consistent in ministry. It would be so easy to put the blame on my overly busy family life and the day-to-day care of my special needs daughter, but I have decided to put the blame on myself, where it belongs. I often fail to depend on God for my ministry needs, so I do only what I think is sufficient. What I need to do instead, is to reach ministerial capacity by setting goals and establishing a strategic marketing plan that identifies my target audience and their needs. Once I realize who my target audience is and what my target audience needs, I should become busy creating products and services to meet the needs of this target audience. For example, analyzing and applying marketing strategies, which are outside the scope of this book, would help me determine whether mentally ill women, homeless women, or women in prison are my target audience and would help me determine the products and services that I should provide for the ministry that I have chosen. Kingdom business is no different from regular business. We must set goals and implement plans which will bring about success for God's Kingdom. God will provide for our ministries when we put plans in place. He is our sufficiency (2 Cor 3:5), and our ministries are all about Him, not about us.

Reflect

Listen to what God is saying to you and me today:

I give you power and set you apart to do the things that I have called you to do (Acts 13:2); The ministry which I entrust to you is not yours, but Mine; You are just a vessel that I am using; Do not worry about delays or timing; I will let you know when the time is right; Hold on to My unchanging hands; I will help you (Ps 46:1); Know Me for yourself; Rely on Me; Do not lean on others; I want to tell you secrets that no one else can tell you (Amos 3:7); Confide in Me; Delight in Me; Worship Me; I am your Savior (Isa 43:3); I am your deliverer (Ps 18:2); Have I ever forsaken you (Josh 1:5)? When you needed a friend, did I abandon you? When you needed comfort, did I leave you comfortless? Look to Me for all your needs; I am able to do much more than you think; Look to Me for big things; I own everything (Ps 89:11); I will supply your needs (Phil 4:19); Do not be afraid; I hold the key to all things (Rev 3:7); Step out in faith and depend on Me for all things; I am your God, your Savior, and your soon coming King (Isa 43:3;1 Cor 1:7).

Respond

Describe your ministry. How are you depending on God for your ministerial needs?

Chapter 25

Have Faith in God

When I think of faith, I think of standing on the promises of God, without questioning God's integrity or God's purposes. For example, faith means trusting that God will deliver you and me from financial hardship and believing that He can and will do it. Faith, to me, is similar to walking on water but not knowing how to swim; putting out my hands to reach the Master, knowing that He is there and knowing that He will prevent me from drowning. Faith is believing in God and knowing that He is in charge of my entire life so I can trust Him for my very existence. The Bible defines faith in Hebrews 11:1 as "being sure of what we hope for and certain of what we do not see." We can believe and have faith in God for healing although we may not see the manifestation of it when we desire it. In this chapter, I will give several examples from the book of Luke to show how Christians, by having faith in God, moved to action and impacted others.

We learned that the angel Gabriel came to Zechariah, Elizabeth's husband, informing him that he will have a son, and that his name would be called John. Elizabeth expressed faith, and believed God for the favor that He had shown her. The fact that Elizabeth had faith to believe in and accept the naming of her child had an impact on her husband Zechariah (Luke 1:1-24, 62-63), because it was at that time he wrote the name "John" on a tablet and God healed him from dumbness.

As another example, Mary, the Mother of Jesus activated her faith by accepting and obeying the sayings of the angel (Luke 1:26-38). Elizabeth's faith had an impact on her cousin Mary. Elizabeth affirmed Mary's conception (Luke 1:42) and solidified her faith when her own baby leaped in her stomach. Mary was filled with the power of God and began to praise the Lord (Luke 1:46-55). The passage in Luke 8:19-20, tells of Mary standing with Jesus' brothers waiting to see Jesus while He preached to a massive crowd. Mary's presence speaks of her faith, for even among the crowd she was waiting to see her Son, Jesus. By being present she had an impact on the crowd who reminded Jesus that they were waiting.

The power of faith was also revealed by a woman in Luke 11:27, who spoke aloud in a crowd blessing Mary, the mother of Jesus, for giving birth and nurturing Jesus. Her faith impacted people standing by, for she spoke highly of Mary and glorified the Lord, Jesus Christ.

Anna, the daughter of "Phanuel, of the tribe of Aser," showed her faith in God by fasting and praying day and night (Luke 2:36). Anna's faith and her prophecy regarding the Christ of Galilee, who would redeem those who will follow Him, had an impact on those who listened. The people understood someone who heard from God and spoke God's truth to them. She was confirming what was already spoken in the Old Testament concerning Jesus who would die and rise again to redeem those from the curse of sin and death.

The woman with the alabaster jar of perfume (Luke 7:36-50), utilized faith by visiting Jesus at the home of a Pharisee. Her faith in Jesus allowed her to disregard what the Pharisees and others thought of her. Her faith allowed her to sit at Jesus' feet, weep in repentance and wipe his feet with her tears and with her hair, kiss his feet and pour perfume on them. Her faith impacted others in the company of Jesus, who recognized that it was faith in Jesus and not prominence that contributed to one's salvation. They realized that the woman came to Jesus as she was, in faith, and humbly knelt and repented of her sin before them all. Her faith was all it took to reach Jesus. I believe that they understood their need for repentance and love for the Savior. The woman's action in approaching Jesus openly and humbly by faith, had an impact on Jesus who said to her, "Your faith has saved you, go in peace" (Luke 7:50).

There was a woman who had been crippled for eighteen years. She was bent over and could not straighten up. Jesus called her and said to her, "Woman you are set free from your infirmity." He put his hands on her and she, utilizing faith, immediately straightened up. Her faith had an impact on the synagogue ruler who was displeased that she was healed on the Sabbath day, but others gave God glory for the good things Jesus had done (Luke 13:10-13).

And finally, the account of Mary Magdalene, Joanna, the mother of James and the other women, is an example of the importance of faith for two reasons: these were the women who by faith, were healed of demonic spirits and other ailments and accompanied Jesus during his public ministry and assisted Him

financially (Luke 8:1-4). These women of faith followed Jesus on the day of his crucifixion (Luke 23:55-56).
They saw where Jesus' body was laid. They returned
in faith, the following day to anoint his body with
spices. They found the stone rolled away, and on
entering the tomb, found that the body was taken
away. Their faith allowed them to enter the tomb in
search of Jesus and to be informed by an angel that
Jesus was raised from the dead and to be the first to
see the risen Lord. Their faith impacted the apostles
and others who they informed of Jesus' resurrection
(Luke 24:10).

Having faith in God is knowing that you can
come to Him as you are, you can have a personal
relationship with Jesus Christ, confess and repent
of your sin and knowing that God loves you and
will forgive you of your sin. Like the Christians who
exercised faith, you can have faith in God and impact
the lives of others.

Reflect

Listen to what God is saying today:

> *Have faith in Me (Mark 11:22); I have not forgotten
> you (Josh 1:5); Your deliverance is on the way (Ps 18:2);
> I will be faithful toward you (Deut 7:9); Whatsoever I*

say, I will do; I am not a man that I should lie (Num 23:19); I am a faithful God (Deut 7:9).

Respond

What tools have you learned from this chapter? How can your faith in God impact the lives of others?

Chapter 26

Walk in the Light

God often sends prophets and others to speak into our lives. Many times, they confirm what God is telling us. On the other hand, we have sometimes been lured by voices that are not God's. Like Job, these voices come from friends or others who want to see us do well. They give advice and suggestions that seem so applicable and so meaningful, but, oftentimes, they are not from God. As a result, we sometimes make decisions that are outside God's will. Yes, we need friends and people in our lives; we need advice, but I believe that the ultimate voice we should seek and obey is the voice of God.

Heeding the voice of God means walking in His light. Throughout my most difficult journey with our daughter Jo-An, people were always giving me advice. When I visited our daughter in the hospital a few years ago, a social worker approached me several times suggesting that I put our daughter in long-term care to make it easy for her to get admittance to a group home. I later learned that our daughter did not qualify for the agency's independent living arrangements, so putting her in long-term care, a locked-down facility, with the hope of obtaining a group home for her, was unrealistic and outside the will of God. God's will is for His children to walk in the light: that is, to live abundant lives of hope, and freedom in Him.

God wants us to live in freedom and hope because He is our Father, and He wants the best for us, His children. He is in the business of forgiving and restoring us to wholeness. God sent his Son to the world to be a light in the midst of darkness and to help those who are lost to turn to the light. In John 8:12 (NIV), Jesus said, "I am the light of the world. Whoever follows Me will never walk in darkness, but will have the light of life." When we believe in and have an intimate relationship with God through Jesus Christ, we hear God's voice. He shows us the way so we can walk in the light of life.

Reflect

God is saying to you and me today:

I have brought you out of darkness into My marvelous light (Isa 42:16); Walk in the light (John 8:12); Do not be lured by many voices; Heed My voice; I have given you freedom, but use it wisely (John 8:36; 1 Pet 2:16-17); In these last days, many will profess My name, but be careful and do not obey the voice of strangers (2 Tim 3:5).

Respond

Describe a situation that has kept you in darkness and prevented you from walking in the light.

Chapter 27

---—※—---

Believe in the God of Yesterday; He Has Not Changed

Every year, I would take a retreat alone, but in 2013, I was busy coordinating our daughter Leah's wedding and was unable to take a retreat then. With three grandchildren, we have many family events, including christenings, first communions, birthday parties and cookouts so we are happily enjoying every moment of our lives. I couldn't wait for the appropriate time to go on my three night retreat. It came in March 2014.

I was finally alone. I could talk to God about my failures and my insecurities, and He would understand. I could cry softly or loudly, and He would wipe away all my tears. I would have more time to read His Word, and He would help me to apply the Word of God to my life and give me hope.

I had reached a desperate point in my life. I wanted to see a change in our daughter Jo-An's situation. She was seeing a specialist and had been on a special diet because the doctor felt she had food allergies. He suggested that we purchase organic vegetables, fruit, meat, and fish. In addition to the constant routine of house cleaning, I was up every morning preparing her breakfast, lunch, and dinner. I kept up with her appointments and made sure that she had an ample supply of supplements, purchasing them from the doctor or from Amazon if she ran out. Her doctor educated me on the essential foods that our daughter needed and I will always be grateful to him for that. I depended on him however, for answers to our daughter's medical condition, but, unfortunately, we found out recently from an allergist that our daughter does not in fact have food allergies and that the supplements that the doctor had prescribed for her were not necessary to maintain her health.

Because I wanted answers immediately and did not wait on God, I landed at the doctor's office putting my hope and trust in him rather than in the big God I serve, Who promises to be with me always (Matt 28:20) and to bear my burdens (Ps 68:19). While I was praying, I sensed that I truly had God in my life, but was going in circles working at everything alone, without totally involving God, Who is always by my side (Ps 139:7-10). I surrendered to God, repented, and cried out to God for help.

After crying out to God, a ray of sunlight filled my room. Could this be God showing me that He is here with me? He has never forsaken me. He is with me in the fire of my life (Ps 23:4). He is with me when nothing seems to go right. He is with me when I cannot seem to find an answer to life's problems. He is my exceeding joy when I am sad (Ps 43:4), and my strength when I am weak (2 Cor 12:9). He is my Provider, my Healer and my Shelter from the storm (Phil 4:19; Ps 103:3; Ps 61:3). He is my Victor, my Daddy, my Father. He has all that I need (Ps 89:11). I must rise up, understand, and know who my Redeemer is and who I am—His child.

I must believe in the God of yesterday, who healed the woman with the issue of blood (Mark 5:25-32). This woman bled for twelve years and had gone to many doctors, but none could cure her. Although she was considered unclean by society's standards, she mustered up her courage, rose up, and left her house when she heard that the Master was in town. She knew who her Redeemer was, and she knew that she could appear before Him just as she was and He would accept her. She applied her faith, pushed her way into the crowd and thought, "If only I could touch the hem of the Master's cloak, I will be healed..."and she was.

I must believe in the God of yesterday, who healed the man who had an infirmity for thirty-eight years (John 5:5-9 NKJV). Jesus asked the man, "Do you want to be made well?" The man answered Him, "Sir, I have no man to put me into the pool when the water is stirred up; but while I am coming, another steps down before me." Jesus said to him, "Rise, take up your bed and walk." The man was healed immediately.

When you and I read the above biblical stories, and the healings that Jesus performed, then and now, we know that we are not alone; God is with us (Ps 46:7) and can take care of the small and big things in our lives. What He did for the woman with the blood condition and the man with the infirmity for thirty-eight years, He will do for you and me, for He is the same God yesterday, today, and forever (Heb 13:8). He has not changed. We must put our situations into His hands and trust Him to work them out. God works things out in His time; we must patiently believe and wait on Him. Jesus Christ has paid the price for your situation and mine (1 Pet 2:24); He will deliver us both (Ps 18:2).

Reflect

Listen to your Father's council:

I am the Lord your God; I am the same God Who brought My people out of the land of Egypt and out of the land of bondage (Exod 20:2); Believe in Me; I am the same God yesterday, today, and forever (Heb 13:8); I have not changed (Mal 3:6); Just as Abraham obeyed Me and his faith was counted for righteousness (Heb 11:8), you also must obey My voice, and Mine only; I am bringing you/ your family member out of bondage and preparing you/ your family member to enter into a land flowing with milk and honey (Num 14:8); I bring healing in my wings to those who revere my name (Mal 4:2); Hope in Me; Your deliverance is near (Ps 18:2).

Respond

What comes to mind as you read this chapter? How are you handling your life issues? What are you believing God for? Explain.

Chapter 28

Look to the Future

*W*hen you are experiencing severe emotional pain, you tend to see a bleak future ahead. Being in a state of bondage, you may feel hopeless and unable to envisage how God can deliver you from your critical situation. God, however, is able to do exceedingly, abundantly more than we can ask or imagine (Eph 3:20). The story of the Samaritan woman found in the Gospel of John 4:1-30, is one that many people can identify with. Before I go into the story, I want to give you background information regarding the Samaritans.

The Samaritans gained strength following the fall of the Northern Kingdom of Israel in 722 BC (2 Kings 17). The Assyrians exiled the Israelites and brought in their own people, who occupied the land,

and worshiped foreign gods alongside the true God. Samaria was the capital city in the north, and the Samaritans' place of worship was Mount Gerizim, while Jerusalem became the city in the south, with the temple at Jerusalem as the Jews' place of worship. This meant that Samaritans and Jews had different forms of worship. This issue of worship will come into play as I make reference to the Samaritan woman and how she viewed worship.

She is an example of someone who, I believe, felt overwhelmed with her life. The Bible does not give a complete background of this woman, so for the sake of discussion, l will paint a picture of her. This woman may have been in her early twenties, had sunken eyes from constant crying, and was sad. She walked hurriedly and briskly to Jacob's well, located near Sychar, a town in Samaria. Jesus arrived there, tired from his journey from Judea, and sat at the well while the disciples went into the town to buy food.

She came to the well at noon and breathed a sigh of relief as she approached the well, because the other women of the village were not in sight; if they had been, they might have asked her questions, forcing her to disclose her private life. She had five husbands, and the man with whom she was currently living was not her husband. In the midst of her anxiety and her hurry, she was startled and utterly amazed to find a man sitting at the well—Jesus. For a moment, fear gripped her, but as she got closer, she didn't feel threatened by His presence. He seemed calm and gentle. He looked Jewish, and, since Jews had no dealings with Samaritans, it was impossible for Him to know anything about her. She looked at the man again and wondered whether she should tell Him her story.

Her story began at the age of ten, when a family friend sexually abused her. After that horrible incident, she experienced fear, self-hate, guilt, shame, and condemnation—embracing a victim mentality. She felt she was never good enough, and, though she tried to have a successful marriage, she could not. In her quest to find love, she left one husband only to be physically and mentally abused by the others, leaving her in a state of rejection, bitterness and unforgiveness. She also suffered with low self-esteem—the aftermath of rejection, fear, and shame. After every divorce, she would continue to search for love, only to be abandoned once more. She was a subject of gossip in her community as everyone stared at her and talked about her. In her confused state, she arrived at the well, and, in a split second, as if this man could read her mind, He talked to her and asked her for a drink of water. All she wanted was to fetch her own water and leave, but the man continued to discuss "water."

To initiate a response from her, Jesus gently asked her for a drink of water. He said to her, "If you knew the gift of God and who it is that asks you for a drink, you would have asked Him, and He would have given you living water" (John 4:10). He used the term "living water," a familiar term used in that day to refer to pure water, even that which was in Jacob's well. He chose "water" because it satisfied one's thirst temporarily, but wanted to communicate that He, Jesus, is the "living water," which would satisfy her eternally. It would not only wash her and make her clean again, but would also give her hope for the future.

Jesus knew her situation: her feeling of hopelessness and the love that she desperately needed. He brought up the issue of worship because she felt strongly that worship should happen at a place, either at Mount Gerizim where her ancestors worshiped or at Jerusalem where Jews worshiped. Jesus wanted her to look to the future, when she would "worship the Father in the Spirit and in Truth" (John 4:23). Prayer, praise, worship, and studying the Bible occur when one accepts Jesus as his/her Lord and Savior. Jesus told her that He was the Messiah that she was waiting for. She accepted Jesus as her Savior that moment and went into the town and told everyone about Jesus, the man who knew everything about her.

In summary, Jesus waited for the Samaritan woman at the well because He knew the emotional pain she was experiencing. He continues to wait for us, His sons and daughters, to come to Him. He knew all about the Samaritan woman's life and how she felt and that she would go to Jacob's well to draw water. He knew that she would receive salvation and, because of her testimony, others would come to a saving knowledge of His grace. He also knows what you and I are experiencing and promises to deliver us and bring us peace.

Although each person's story is different, everyone can identify with some aspect of the Samaritan woman's story. Like the Samaritan woman, some of us mask our true feelings to hide our past and our current struggles. We fail to deal with our situations; we put them off thinking that they will go away, but they do not. We will not find solutions to our problems until we encounter Jesus and discuss the matter with Him. Maybe you are currently experiencing difficulty in your marriage, grieving the death of a loved one or facing the incarceration of your son or daughter. It's time to confess, repent, renounce your past and forgive those who have done you wrong or put you through a test. Ask God to forgive you for holding onto your past. Put your past situation to rest and look to the future. God has provided you with renewed life through the death and resurrection of His Son, Jesus Christ (Rom 5:10).

Reflect

The Lord is saying to you and me right now, regardless of how we feel:

Look no more to the past, but look to the future (Isa 43:18; Jer 29:11); Prepare yourself; Pray as never before; Don't you know that I am God (Ps 100:3)? You can do all things in Me (Phil 4:13); I will deliver you from your peril (Ps 18:2); Stand on My promises and look to the future; I will make a way for you (Isa 43:19); Be patient; I will open the doors (Isa 43:19; Isa 54:2); Daughter/Son, rise up from the ash heap and put on a garment of praise; I died so you can have life (Rom 5:17); Be confident; Be strong.

Respond

Have you experienced life issues similar to that of the Samaritan woman, such as childhood abuse, a separation, a divorce or an unhealthy relationship that did not work out and which has left you feeling angry, lonely, rejected, bitter, and unforgiving? Describe your issue(s) here. What have you learned from reading the Samaritan woman's story?

Chapter 29

Be Still before God

Being still before God is a discipline that every Christian should practice. Most Christians believe that being busy for God is the way to operate. While being on the battlefield and doing kingdom work is rewarding and pleasing to God, God also wants our attention. God delights in the praises of His people. God speaks to us audibly, through our dreams, through His Word, and through His prophets. When we are still, we hear His voice.

The familiar story of Mary and Martha found in the Gospel according to Luke 10:38-42, illustrates how to be still before God. Jesus visited the home of two sisters, Mary and Martha. Mary sat at Jesus' feet and heard His word, while Martha was busy cleaning and serving. Martha was worried that she was the one who was serving and not her sister, but Jesus replied to her, "Martha, Martha, thou art careful and troubled about many things. But one thing is needful and Mary hath chosen that good part, which shall not be taken away from her."

Like Mary, we need to choose the good part—to sit at Jesus' feet, to hear from Him, and to learn from Him. He tells us secrets, guides us, teaches us, blesses us, cares for us, and plants our feet on solid ground. When we are busy, we are unable to hear God's voice; we operate on our own without His guidance.

Being still before God allows you and me to answer the following questions: What are my priorities? Am I placing God first in my life? Where am I in my personal walk with God? Do I need to repent and ask for God's forgiveness for any wrongdoing? What does God expect of me in regard to my relationships? Am I loving and treating others with kindness? Am I walking in my purpose? What task does God have in mind for me to do? Why does He want me to do this? When is the time frame for this ministry? How does God want me to do this? Where is God planning on implementing this ministry? Who would God send as my helpers? The list goes on.... Only God can guide us, but we should cease from our busyness and listen to His voice. Being busy in the past has cost me considerable time and energy. The cost is not spending enough time with God. Now, I have chosen to be still before God, to listen to Him as He molds me and fashions me into that vessel fit for use in His Kingdom and for His glory.

Reflect

God is saying to you and me today:

I have seen your toil; I know that you have faith in Me; Wait patiently; The time is coming when you will see My hand at work in your life; I am the Lord; That is My name (Ps 100:3); I exist forever and ever (Rev 4:10); I have kept covenants with men and women in the past (Gen 17:9); I will keep My covenant with you (Num 23:19); Your entire family will receive salvation and restoration for many generations to come (Acts 16:31); Be still and know that I am God (Ps 46:10).

Respond

Are you a Martha or a Mary? What has busyness cost you or what have you learned from sitting at Jesus' feet? Describe.

Chapter 30

Give of Yourself Freely

On Friday, May 30, 2014, my phone rang. Thinking that someone needed prayer, I stopped praying and picked up the telephone, only to hear from a person who seemed self-centered and manipulative. The person kept on talking about what I needed to do and why I needed to do it. I was getting a headache and was forced to cut the conversation short. It is so important to connect with the right people and not be coerced by someone who has his or her own agenda. Later, I learned that the person has had a serious problem and was not open to seeking help. Her situation is troubling for everyone with whom she has been in contact. I could have used my time more effectively by helping someone who needed my help. God has called you and me to help those who cannot help themselves. We can help the poor children of the world.

Poverty occurs locally as well as worldwide, and, therefore, you and I can find ways to help the needy. By contributing to local charities that are already doing the work, we provide poor children with basic resources, such as food, water, shelter, clothing, and educational resources so they can have access to quality education. The startling statistics on hunger and death confirm the reality of poverty.

Children who are victims of poverty suffer from hunger, which leads to malnutrition. The United Nations Food and Agricultural Organization estimated that nearly 870 million people of the 7.1 billion people in the world, or one in eight, suffered from chronic undernourishment from 2010-2012. World Hunger poverty facts and statistics for 2013 show that children from poorer regions tend to fall into this category. For example, more than 70 percent of malnourished children live in Asia, 26 percent in Africa and 4 percent in Latin America and the Caribbean. Many of these undernourished children become ill and die. Children who are poorly nourished suffer up to 160 days of illness each year. Poor nutrition plays a role in at least half of the 10.9 million child deaths each year. Children and their families live in deplorable conditions, oftentimes without a place to live, without proper clothing or suitable drinking water.

We can show compassion to people in small ways. I remember my mother, Agnes, and the compassion she showed to children and youth passing by who were drenched from the rain which fell heavily in the village where we lived on the Island of Trinidad and Tobago. She provided the children with a change of clothing and some hot soup and sent them on their way home. Those were acts of kindness.

The following story describes other acts of kindness. When I attended seminary, I met a Haitian minister, who, in 2013, was convinced that he would return to Haiti to help his people who had been hit by the horrible earthquake which killed thousands in 2010. He arranged a mission trip and began the long road of raising funds. I had the honor of attending one of his fundraising concerts and witnessed an elderly lady who walked to the podium and donated $1500, the money she had put aside for her funeral. This minister took his wife and children to Haiti to feed "the broken ones," the poor children of Haiti. He returned to Haiti in 2014. We may not all be able to go on a mission trip, but we can contribute money, food, or clothing to organizations that help the poor.

Reflect

Here what the Lord is saying to you and me today:

Let prayer, worship, and the Word be your priority; Walk in newness of life; This is your time to live; Feed the hungry and clothe the naked; Freely you have received, freely you should give (Matt 10:8); Call on people you have not seen or heard from; Live like tomorrow is your last; Remember, I said to you whatever you experience, it is for your good (Rom 8:28); If someone hates you, remember I love you (Eph 2:4); Do not give up on yourself or on others; Let forgiveness and love be your tools for life; Love unconditionally; Live life fearlessly knowing that I will protect you (Ps 91:4); Forgive mercifully, knowing that your Father in heaven forgives you (Matt 6:14).

Respond

Explain ways that you are giving of yourself freely?

Chapter 31

Have the Right Motive

For years, I focused on seminary training believing that this training will prepare me to be ordained at a local church. I was looking for a title, although I was already doing the work of a minister: speaking at Christian Resource Network Breakfast meetings, conducting monthly breakfast round table sessions, participating in prayer and support groups, as well as conducting workshops, seminars, and women's retreats. I became an active member of a church for several years, hoping that I would obtain a ministerial license. I had become a people-pleaser rather than a God-pleaser. I reasoned that if I were ordained, people would recognize my ability. God was not pleased with my motive. He wanted me to have the right motive—a motive to please Him, and to love others as He loves them.

Ministry takes on many different forms, but it is about loving others and taking the Gospel of Jesus Christ to those who are lost. Some people are missionaries, some are apostles, prophets, pastors, teachers, or evangelists. Some ministries focus on outreaches to the homeless on the streets or in shelters, to the mentally ill, to the sick in hospitals and to those in prison. They provide food, clothing, blankets and Bibles for people in need. Ministries like these are doing a great work and are answering the charge given in the passage taken from the Gospel of Matthew 25:31-40 NKJV:

"When the Son of Man comes in His glory, and all the angels with Him, He will sit on his glorious throne. All the nations will be gathered before Him, and He will separate the people one from another as a shepherd separates the sheep from the goats. He will put the sheep on His right and the goats on His left. Then the King will say to those on His right, 'Come, you who are blessed by My Father; take your inheritance, the kingdom prepared for you since the creation of the world. For I was hungry and you gave Me something to eat, I was thirsty and you gave Me something to drink, I was a stranger and you invited Me in, I needed clothes and you clothed Me, I was sick and you looked after Me, I was in prison and you came to visit Me.' Then the righteous will answer Him, 'Lord, when did we see You hungry and feed You, or thirsty and give You something to drink? When did we see You a stranger and invite You in, or needing clothes and clothe You? When did we see You sick or in prison and go to visit You?' The King will reply, 'Truly I tell you, whatever you did for one of the least of these brothers and sisters of Mine, you did for Me.'"

The aforementioned verses show how ministries to the poor, the homeless and the lost touch God's heart and confirm that the purpose of every ministry is to advance God's Kingdom by being a witness and showing love to others through giving. Giving also includes spending time with the elderly who are left without families, giving to your favorite charity, and much more.

God spoke to me about starting a ministry to my family and extended family, but I kept putting it off. I wondered if people would show up or if I would end up wasting my time. At the time of this writing, I have opened my doors for prayer and my family as well as my extended family met on several occasions.

Now, I am excited about serving others through prayer and Bible-study. Serving others makes a difference in their lives, and God gets the glory out of our lives. We must serve others out of love and not out of a motive to advance ourselves.

Do you have the right motive? Are you in ministry to satisfy your ego and impress others? If so, I want to encourage you to change your perspective. Have the right motive. You are special, unique to God, and God wants to take that unique gift that He has given you and use it to expand His Kingdom. Do not look at the gift that someone else has. No two people are alike, and God has given each person a unique gift to do a special task on this earth. Each of us should be happy with the gift and the task that God has assigned to each one of us. Let us take the challenge, rise up, and change our world.

Reflect

Listen to what God is saying to you and me today:

I am not interested in form or fashion, but in the demonstration of your love to your loved ones and others (1 John 3:23); Have the right motive by modeling the love of God to others; Stop being busy and show love; I am a

God of the impossible (Matt 19:26), and I can change your circumstances (Dan 2:21); Count your life worthy of Christ, Who suffered and died and brought Himself to a point of no reputation for your sake (Phil 2:7-8).

Respond

What is your motive in ministry? Describe.

Prayer of Salvation

....That if you confess with your mouth Jesus as Lord, and believe in your heart that God raised Him from the dead, you will be saved (Rom 10:9 NASB).

Lord God of the Universe,
Creator of everything,
I come to you in desperation,
Desiring to have an intimate relationship with You
And to invite Jesus Christ to be my Lord and Savior.

I confess and repent of my sins
And ask for Your forgiveness.
I accept Jesus as my Lord and Savior,
The One who died on the cross and rose again,
Paying the penalty for my sins,
So I could receive salvation and eternal life.
I pray this in Jesus' name, Amen.

By Joan M. Blake (2010)

CPSIA information can be obtained
at www.ICGtesting.com
Printed in the USA
BVOW06*2317060117

472290BV00014B/5/P